Steve Milano & Associates, LLC
www.managingcorporatefatigue.com

Steve Milano

Copyright ©2012-2019 Steve Milano & Associates, LLC
All Rights Reserved

Second Edition

ISBN 978-1727281873

Printed in United States of America

Managing Corporate Fatigue

How to Reduce Physical and Mental Stress Through Habit and Lifestyle Changes

Contents

Foreword

Chapter 1 – Sleep is More Important Than you Realize - 1

Chapter 2 – Eating for Productivity - 28

Chapter 3 – Maintaining Energy Levels in the Workplace - 52

Chapter 4 – Managing (not Eliminating) Stress - 73

Chapter 5 – Why Routines Help - 95

Chapter 6 – What's your Work/Home Air Quality Like? - 99

Chapter 7 – Managing the Flu (You're Going to Get it) - 103

Tips for Dealing With a Hangover - 110

Putting it all Together - 112

Foreword

You can't undo the damage.

"I'm just going to work these hours until I make partner, then I'll slow down and take care of myself."

"This project is only going to last a few months. I'll get extra sleep on the weekends and then work regular hours after the project is over."

Sorry, your body doesn't work that way. The type of damage you do working long hours is permanent and can't be reversed.

Let's say you have to make a road trip that's going to take you eight hours of driving by yourself.

You decide that you can probably go 90 mph on this particular four-lane highway without getting pulled over. You haven't changed the oil or air filter lately, but if you see the temperature gauge starting to get too hot, you'll just drop your speed down to 55 mph and you'll be able to keep going.

That's because driving 55 mph won't cause any new damage to your engine, and since your car is still running, the stress you were putting on the engine going 90 mph for hours didn't do any permanent damage.

Sorry, but you can't undo the damage you did to your engine those past several hours by driving at a more reasonable speed now. Sure, you might put off breaking down for 30 minutes or so, but it's too late to undo the damage you've already done to your vehicle.

That's how your body and brain work.

If you flood your body with stress hormones each day, kill brain cells with a lack of sleep each night, and damage your organs for years, you can't reverse all that damage by taking better care of yourself at some point in the future.

You won't do any new damage to yourself after you slow down and take care of yourself, but your body will still break down years earlier from the damage you previously did to it.

By slowing down "later," you might put off sitting in a wheelchair attached to an oxygen tank and developing dementia by a few years, but you'll still pay the price for those years you spent killing brain cells and weakening your organs and other tissues.

Here's what happens when you say, "I'm just going to work these hours until I make partner, then I'll slow down and take care of myself."

What happens when you make partner? Do partners work 9 to 5 with no stress? Do they get eight hours of sleep each night, eat a healthy diet and get regular exercise?

Physical and mental stress among high-performing, high-stress workers rarely, if ever, comes to a complete stop.

What is Corporate Fatigue?

Corporate Fatigue is the combination of physical, mental and productivity problems that arise from working many hours on a regular basis, often under stress.

CF is caused by a lack of proper sleep, poor workplace eating habits, lack of physical activity at the office and mental stress that increases the release of specific hormones that cause physical damage.

Health Problems Caused by CF

- Suppressed immune system
- Premature aging
- Sleep disorders
- Heart disease
- Stroke
- Hypertension
- Obesity

Work Problems Caused by CF

- Reduce cognitive function
- More work product mistakes
- Missed deadlines
- Less creativity (breakthroughs and solutions)
- Increased absenteeism (illness)
- Increased presenteeism (lethargy)
- Employees coming in to work sick
- Employees spreading illness
- Higher staff turnover

Emotional Problems Caused by CF

- Irritability
- Anger
- Relationship problems
- Depression
- Substance abuse
- Career burnout

General Wellness vs. Performance Wellness

Most work-related wellness books and seminars focus on improving your overall health and wellness—but you already know you should be eating healthy, doing some regular exercise and getting a good night's sleep.

Wellness that improves your performance has a different focus. This book focuses on how to sleep better at night, eat specifically during the workday and add physical activity (vs. exercise) to your daily routine to improve your performance at work.

If you're going to work long hours on a regular basis, you unfortunately can't eliminate CF or the long-term damage it does to your brain and body.

However, using a variety of personalized lifestyle and workplace habits, you can reduce some of the damage you do to yourself.

You don't need to make major lifestyles changes to make major improvements to your health. Small but regular changes in your daily habits are easy to make and can pay huge dividends.

These changes can help you become more alert, creative and productive each hour you work. You'll be less likely to develop irritability, anger, depression, high blood pressure, heart attack, stroke and other physical and mental problems.

This book is filled with tips for improving your eating, sleeping, fitness and stress-management habits.

You don't need to eat tofu and sprouts, meditate and chant or exercise for 90 minutes each day to completely change your life for the better.

Working long hours each week will catch up with you. This book—or any other—can't change that. This book can help you reduce the amount damage CF will cause you in the short-term and help delay the long-term damage that comes from abusing your body by spending many hours each week under stress while getting less than eight hours of sleep per night.

This book gives you overviews of areas of your life you can modify—not completely change—to improve your business performance and personal life.

- If you can't get eight hours of sleep, there are ways to improve the sleep you get.

- If you're going to eat at fast-food restaurants, there are ways to do it so it's not as unhealthy.

- There are ways to get meaningful exercise without going to the gym.

- There are ways to reduce your stress levels without yoga and TM.

It would be great if you could commit to serious diet, fitness, sleep and stress-management efforts, but if you feel this isn't realistic for you, modifying (but not completely changing) your working and lifestyle habits can still change your life.

If you can't live healthy, at least fthe live healthier.

It's easier than you think, will make you more productive and successful in business and life, can help you ward off diseases, dangerous health conditions and even death for a few more years . . . and might even be fun for you.

Chapter I:
Sleep is More Important than you Realize

Normally, a wellness book would begin with healthy eating, then move to exercise, then cover stress management, and then you might get some tips on sleep and work/life balance.

However, more and more research shows that a sleep deficit can be as damaging, or even more damaging, to your work performance than poor diet and lack of exercise.

It will also do significant long-term damage to your health and cause you to age prematurely.

And, you can't "bank" sleep on the weekends or just deprive yourself for a few months or years while you finish a project, manage a case or climb the corporate ladder.

Some of the damage caused by sleep deprivation is permanent.

That's why it's important to start this book talking about one of the least understood and most damaging aspects of working too hard.

The Basics

We all know you need to get a good night's sleep if you want to perform your best, but what does that mean, "good night's sleep"?

Your life basically occurs in three stages as they relate to your physical and mental growth and decline.

Age 1-20 – Your body is in growth stage
Age 20-40 – Your body is in repair and regenerate stage
Age 40-60 – Your body is in maintenance and preservation stage

Your body is made up of trillions of cells, and it protects and repairs those cells in different ways, based on your stage of life.

From birth until the age of about 20, your body focuses on growth, creating new cells.

From about age 20 to 40, your body works to repair and regenerate its cells.

After age 40, your body starts allowing unused or unimportant cells to die. It begins putting its energy into repairing the most-used, most-important cells. This is the start of the aging process and what eventually leads to non-traumatic deaths, or death by natural causes.

Diet helps fuel your body and provides nutrients for cell growth and repair.

Exercise helps build muscles, maintains health and as you get older, alerts your brain that these cells you're using are important and should be maintained.

Sleep is the time when most of your growth, repair and regeneration of cells occurs.

Good sleep is sleep that has a repairing and restorative effect on your body and brain.

Have you ever thought about what your body is doing when you sleep? We often think that when we're sleeping, we're basically doing nothing. During sleep, however, your body works to keep you healthy by performing certain "repair projects"...

- Repairs tissue (increased growth hormone production)
- Repairs nerve cells
- Neutralizes neurotoxins
- Replenishes depleted chemicals
- Strenghtens immune system
- Improves long-term memory
- Raises and lowers blood pressure

If you sleep properly, you go through several different stages of sleep, during which your body and brain perform different repair and restore projects.

As stated earlier, your body is comprised of trillions of cells. That's trillion with a "t." During the day, your normal physical activities stress and damage these cells. Your body is a very self-healing mechanism, so it works to repair or replace these cells.

An example of your body being self-healing is what happens when you cut yourself. Your body rushes morphine to the area to reduce the pain, sends clotting agents to stop the bleeding, forms a scab to protect the wound while it begins healing, and forms scar tissue to replace the skin that was cut.

Sleep is another example of how your body works to self-heal, specifically repairing the cells you stress and damage during the day.

General Health & Wellness Effects of Poor Sleep

Lack of sleep has negative impacts on your:

- Brain
- Immune system
- Heart
- Weight
- Mental health

It can lead to:

- Decreased cognitive function
- Obesity
- Alcoholism
- Substance abuse
- Relationship problems
- Depression
- Irritability
- Anger

Rats deprived of sleep in experiments show:

- Fewer white blood cells—the body's main defense against infection
- Inferior healing capacities
- Inability to maintain a stable body temperature
- Skin lesions
- Loss of body mass

The rats ultimately died of sepsis or just "exhaustion."

Sleep-deprived humans show less than half of the protective antibodies of people who get adequate sleep.

Work Quantity vs. Work Quality

When it comes to pulling all-nighters, there may be times you don't have a choice. But if you regularly work on only a few hours of sleep, you'll decrease the quantity and quality of the work you do each day and begin to damage your brain and body.

The hours of extra work you put in when you're tired not only are less valuable than those you perform when you're adequately rested, but you'll also increase your risk of an error, which can result in a lost client or financial damage to your company.

So, 12 hours of work on five hours of sleep isn't necessarily better for your company than 10 hours of work on eight hours of sleep.

The quality of hours you put in each day outweighs the quantity of hours you work.

Hormones are What Does It

I used to spend the night at a friend's apartment in Chicago and the room I slept in was awful for trying to sleep. The room overlooked one of the city's busiest intersections, where five high-traffic streets met. Directly underneath the window of this second-floor apartment was a bus stop. All night long, buses would whoosh into the stop, open their doors, discharge and take on passengers, then whoosh away.

Across the street was a pay-before-you-pump gas station. New customers would try to start pumping and the clerk would get on the loudspeaker and blast, "Sir, you need to come inside and pay first!" jolting me out of bed.

And it got worse. On the windowsill, about 10 feet from my head, pigeons would congregate, softly cooing. The windows had sheer curtains that, combined with a skylight, inundated the room with bright sunshine each morning. Let's not even talk about how uncomfortable the bed was.

Despite all of these impediments to sound sleep, I woke up refreshed and ready to run a marathon each morning. I couldn't understand it. I usually hated getting up each morning. I slammed my hand on the alarm clock to shut it up. I walked to the bathroom with my eyes closed, mumbling under my breath. I dreaded facing the coming commute.

Why did I feel so good then, whenever I slept at my friend's apartment?

My friend had an idea: "I have a theory that if you wake up in a room with sunlight, you wake up feeling better."

So I tried it. The next night, back in my apartment, I left my window shade open a bit before I went to bed. I preferred sleeping and waking in a pitch-dark room, but I gave it a try.

Sure enough, the next morning I awoke without the usually grogginess and irritability I usually experienced when I woke. I didn't hate my boss, job or clients that morning.

What happened?

For most of human history, man did not have light — not even fire. As humans evolved physiologically during our history, whenever our eyes saw darkness coming, our brains registered it as a signal to sleep. So after dark, we went into our caves and slept. When it got dark, our brains released the hormone melatonin to help us sleep better. As our brains experienced sunlight the next morning, the melatonin production slowed so we were no longer sleepy.

When you wake in a pitch-dark room, your brain is swimming in melatonin because it thinks you want to keep sleeping. You wake up drowsy, groggy, irritable and not in a positive mood to start you day. You shave, shower, brush your teeth or dress with your eyes half open. You might dread going into work and want to get back into bed.

If, on the other hand, you wake up in a brightly lit room, your brain will have slowed melatonin production and you are more likely to get out of bed refreshed and ready to go.

This simple lifestyle change can make a huge difference in your quality of life.

Yes, trying to sleep with sunlight in your eyes is no fun, so consider how you'll arrange your curtains to light your room each morning. If it's still dark outside when you get up in the morning, purchase a lamp with a timer that slowly turns on, raising the room's light level 15 minutes or so before you want to wake.

What are These Hormones Doing?

Melatonin isn't the only hormone that's involved in sleep changes.

Your body produces and/or releases more of several hormones during sleep. Some of these hormones, like melatonin, help you get into and stay asleep.

Adrenaline revs you up, so your body produces less of this hormone during sleep.

During sleep, growth hormones are released into the bloodstream for muscle and tissue repair.

Vasopressin helps reduces the need to urinate while you're sleeping.

Sleep also balances appetite. Good sleep results in hunger the next morning (due to glycogen burning during the night). Lack of sleep can result poor insulin regulation, a lack of leptin and an increase in ghrelin, which regulate hunger.

Oxytocin helps with sleep and dreaming, peaking after five hours. You work out problems during sleep, so if you don't get proper sleep, this can affect your mental health.

Progesterone helps with body temperature regulation, which affects your sleep.

One of the biggest hormonal changes caused by sleep is the reduction of the stress hormone cortisol in your blood. Cortisol does many bad things to your body and brain as you'll find out in shortly.

Now you understand why sleep is more than just doing nothing.

You don't need to understand all of these hormonal processes, but you can see there's a lot going on in your body when you sleep—and these processes need to occur each night if you want to maintain your health and put off aging.

The point of this list is to help you understand that sleep is not just "resting" or "doing nothing." It's the time when your body changes its physiological processes to help repair you every night.

If you don't get enough good sleep, your body will start to break down and you'll get old before your time.

You Can't Bank Sleep

We now know from multiple, credible research sources that not getting a full-night's sleep damages brain cells and permanently kills some of them.

We also know that you cannot reverse this process by "banking" sleep on weekends or breaking your sleep into short phases, such as taking power naps during the day.

If you kill brain cells Monday through Friday, you can't re-animate them on Saturday and Sunday.

Just because you sleep 10 or 12 hours on Saturday or Sunday doesn't mean you didn't permanently destroy many of your brain cells Monday through Friday, week after week, month after month, year after year.

A 2017 Swedish study suggests that sleeping in on weekends may help increase lifespan (quantity, but not quality) by several years. The study does not imply that sleeping in on the weekend addresses the damage you do to your brain and body if you don't get enough sleep Monday through Friday.

So, what's the difference between getting six hours of sleep during the week and getting eight hours?

Fifty percent more cortisol in the bloodstream. That's bad. You'll learn why in the stress chapter of this book.

When a group of pilots slept six hours or less for seven nights while on duty, their cortisol levels increased significantly and stayed elevated for two days, according to a study at Germany's Institute for Aerospace Medicine.

Different Types of Sleep

When you sleep, your body goes through 90-minute cycles that take you through different types of sleep. You'll experience Rapid Eye Movement sleep and three to four stages of Non-REM sleep.

REM sleep is the stage of sleep when you have the most intense brain wave activity, similar to when you're awake. Your heart rate and blood pressure rise and your eyes dart around. This is the stage where you dream. This is where you try to work out, solve and deal with problems.

Ever have the dream where you're late for something? Or it's the last day of the semester and you realize you haven't shown up for class and have to take the final? Or the dream where you're nude or barely clothed in public?

If so, you're trying to work out problems you're having with your finances, job security, relationships or other issues.

There are also different conclusions about whether or not you go through memory consolidation during REM sleep. This means that your memories become long-term, and this is important as we get older.

Non-REM sleep makes up about 75 percent of your sleep. During Non-REM sleep, your body slows down. Your brain waves are slower, your breathing slows, your heart rate, body's core temperature and blood pressure all lower.

There are four different stages of NREM sleep, but we don't need to go through those here. You just need to know that all of these stages of sleep are equally important, that you go through all of the cycles roughly every 90 minutes during a full-night's sleep, and because each stage has a different restorative function, you need to get a full-night's sleep

Athletes and children, who have different body growth and repair needs than the average adult, spend more time in Stage 3 non-REM sleep. This is the deep sleep stage where it's difficult for people to wake you.

See how your body knows who you are and what you need at different points in your life?

Are you an Early Bird or a Night Owl?
Some people love to get to the office early, doing their best work before most people have even arrived. Other people are still half asleep at their desk until 10:00 am, finding their stride later and working at a feverish pace late at night.

A brain hormone may play a role in when you work best.

Noradrenaline, also known as norepinephrine, helps stimulate your bodily functions. Some people produce more noradrenaline in the morning, while others produce more at night. Research suggests that most people fall in between these two extremes, performing their best during normal working hours. But if you feel you're an early bird or night owl, now you know why.

If you like to sleep in on the weekends, you're not necessarily lazy. If you can't work late at night, you're not a wimp. We all have productive periods during the day. Two people may be able to work the exact number of hours at the exact level of peak performance, even though one starts early in the morning and the other works more during the evening.

If you have an extreme circadian rhythm, or body clock, and feel your best very early in the morning or very late at night, understand and respect this phenomenon. Save important tasks for your peak periods and take breaks or do lighter work during your low-energy times.

Let key co-workers know your preferences so you can schedule your contribution to the team when you are performing at your best. For example, if you are a night owl, you may want to schedule less-important internal meetings during morning hours, conducting important client research or analyses late at night when you are peaking. Let your co-workers know you'd rather do a less-important breakfast meeting than a dinner outing if you have an important project you need to finish that night. If you're an early bird, schedule breakfast meetings for important tasks or review sensitive documents when you first get into the office.

Power Napping

Many cultures include afternoon naps in their daily routine to help maintain good health. During late afternoon, when outdoor temperatures are highest, some populations siesta for an hour or two after a large lunch.

Penn State University researchers found that a midday snooze cut cortisol levels in subjects who'd lost sleep the previous night. Napping can also help you maintain better energy levels during the day. This is helpful, but doesn't make up for the other damage you do when you don't get eight hours of uninterrupted sleep.

You don't need to lie down and take a 30-minute or hour-long snooze to benefit from napping. If you know you're going to be working late, tell your assistant to hold your calls, then close your office door and turn out the lights for 15 minutes and grab a nap in your chair. If you're making a cross-town cab trip back from a client, turn off your cell phone and catch a few Zs in the cab. Depending on how many time zones you'll be changing during a flight and which direction you'll be traveling, you may be better served by a nap during your flight than an extra 30 minutes of computer work.

If you are a manager and you are asking an employee or group of workers to work late into the night or pull an all-nighter, set up a time during the day for them to take a nap. They'll wake up refreshed and be more productive and able to stay up later during crunch time.

Some people hate naps. Instead of waking up refreshed, they experience headaches, grogginess, prolonged drowsiness and irritability. This could come from a number of reasons, such as very little sleep or too much sleep the night before; restless sleep due to stress; trying to sleep in a lit room; or a nap that's too short or too long.

If you don't like napping, don't give up on this important productivity tool. Experiment at home on the weekends to see if you can determine what type of napping will help you. You may need a minimum of 30 minutes, need to nap in a dark room or nap only after you've had a good night's sleep.

One of the benefits of taking the train into work may be that you catch an extra 30 to 60 minutes of sleep each morning. If you can nap both ways, you might be able to add up to two hours of sleep to your daily routine. If it's your turn to drive the car pool, ask who wants to nap and let them know you aren't offended if they don't chat with you during your ride into the office.

Just remember, napping is a performance tool and does not make up for, or undo the damage from, a lack of a full-night's sleep.

Regulate Your Light Source

Have you ever attended a lecture or presentation that included a slide show or PowerPoint presentation? What happened after the speaker asked for the room lights to be turned down so the audience could see the screen better? If you didn't soon become groggy, you probably noticed others in the audience passing out. This is because of the brain's reaction to darkness — increased melatonin production to help you sleep.

As noted earlier, the amount of light your eyes register affects the amount of melatonin your body produces, and that makes you sleepy.

If you're giving a talk with a video component, don't turn out the lights in the room. Turn off only the lights above the screen. If you won't be able to do that, put less information on each slide so you can use a larger type size and bold face letters that will be easier to read in a lit room. Put black letters on a white background so your white slides will add some light to the room.

At home, set your curtains to ensure you have sunlight in your room when you wake. If you can't do that, consider a sleep lamp that turns on at a time you set.

Bring a sleep mask on work trips to use during flights and at hotels with curtains or drapes that let too much light in at night. Use a sleep mask at home if you have light from a parking lot light or neighbor's home streaming into your room.

Regulate Your Room Temperature

Research suggests that a cooler room may help promote sleep. When you sleep, your body lowers its core temperature. This means sleeping in a cooler room may help you sleep better.

Keep your room between 60 and 67 degrees F, recommends the National Sleep Foundation. Sleeping in a room colder than that may cause restlessness. If you share a room with someone who prefers it warm, try to compromise. You may need to sleep under only a sheet, rather than a blanket, while your partner may need to sleep in pajamas, a sweatshirt or other clothing.

If you are on a plane, skip using a blanket and use the overhead air conditioning nozzle if that won't irritate you.

Although your body lowers it overall temperature when you sleep, the temperature in your hands and feet rises. If you want to sleep when you fly, don't take your shoes off and put a blanket on your body. That's the opposite of what you should do. Sleep with shoes on and with no blanket or jacket. Wear synthetic, rather than cotton socks when you sleep to keep your feet dry.

Dealing with Jet Lag

Traveling across time zones can disrupt your body clock. This is truer when you change more than one or two time zones and spend more than a day or two out of town. Jet lag can produce sluggishness, drowsiness, decreased concentration, lack of alertness and reduce memory function.

For most people, traveling from New York to L.A. or vice versa for a day or two isn't that big a deal in terms of your overall productivity. You may be a bit drowsy when you arrive, have trouble falling asleep that first night or be tired when you wake up the next morning, but you can probably fight through this for the short time you're out of town with no ill effect.

International travel creates more serious jet lag issues.

Flying East to West

If arrive in L.A. at 8:00 pm, that means it's 11:00 pm in New York. You may be tired and ready for bed at 8:00 pm PST.

If you respect your current body clock and go to bed at 11:00 pm EST (8:00 pm PST), waking up at 8:00 am the next morning, you'll have slept 12 hours. Many people who sleep this long feel extremely sluggish and lethargic. If you wake up naturally after eight hours of sleep, you'll wake up at 5:00 a.m. PST. This will cause you to become sleepy again around 8:00 pm that evening.

If you sleep during your flight, you won't be as sleepy when you arrive at 8:00 pm. This will help you stay awake until 11:00 pm PST (your new bed time). The trick is getting the right amount of sleep. Three hours might be too much. If you sleep two hours, waking just before you land, this might help you stay awake.

East-to-West Travel Tips

- Sleep without a blanket to let your body lower its core temperature naturally, as it does when you sleep. You may fall asleep quicker and go into a deeper sleep.

- Wrap a blanket around your feet if the floor is drafty.

- Close the window or wear a mask to block light.

- Stay hydrated. You become dehydrated during flights because of the cabin air. People mistake dehydration for hunger and eat more.

- Eat at least three hours before your in-flight nap. Eat more complex carbohydrates.

- Exercise several hours before you depart.

- Avoid caffeine and alcohol, which lead to dehydration.

Flying West to East

When you travel from the West Coast to the East Coast, you often arrive early in the morning. If your flight arrives as 1:00 a.m., EST, your body may feel like it's only 11:00 pm. If you've slept on the plane, it might seem even earlier and you'll have trouble getting to sleep when you finally arrive home. When you attempt to get up at 8:00 am, you body might feel like it's still 5:00 am.

Even if you take a day flight, you might still have trouble getting to sleep later that night. When it's 11:00 pm EST, your body may still feel likes it's only 8:00 pm. If you slept on your flight, it might be even more difficult to get to sleep.

After a west-to-east flight, performing rigorous exercise during the afternoon or early evening may help you expend energy and sleep better that evening.

If you get home during the day and want to stay awake, get out of your cab several blocks before your office or home and walk the final distance, raising your heart rate and metabolism. This will be especially helpful if it's a sunny day.

If you can have breakfast outdoors in the sunlight in L.A. before you leave for the East Coast, this might help you feel less sluggish when you arrive home than if you spend your West Coast morning hours in a cool, dark room.

It may be a good idea to sleep when it's nighttime in your destination zone. For example, if it's 9:00 pm PST while you're on your flight, it's 12:00 midnight in New York. You may want to sleep on your flight.

If you can get several hours of sleep, wake up after your plane lands, then quickly get back to sleep when you get home, it might be OK to "bank" some sleep hours on your flight. If you will be wired after you wake up from an in-flight nap, unable to get back to sleep after you arrive home from the airport, then avoid a nap. In this scenario, you might get home at 2:00 am and then have to get up after only four or five hours of sleep. Try banking sleep hours earlier in the day when you are on the West Coast to help you make up for this deficit.

West-to-East Travel Tips

- Nap before you fly if you're arriving during the day.

- Open your window shades if you're flying during the day.

- Eat during your flight if you're arriving during the day.

- Get outside in the warm and sunlight before you fly if you're flying during the day.

- Exercise after arriving if you're arriving during the day.

- Nap during the flight if you're arriving during the evening (if you won't be wired afterwards).

- Exercise before departing if you're arriving during the evening.

Do you Have a Sleep Disorder?

Do you ever have days where you could just fall asleep wherever you are? You might be at your desk, riding an elevator, waiting in line or participating in a meeting, and you could just lie down on the floor and pass out right there.

Does this sleepiness ever occur after you've had eight hours of sleep?

This condition is known as hypersomnia and has several causes, including being overweight, lack of sleep or sleep apnea.

If you have sleep apnea, it's a condition that occurs during sleep when you stop breathing. If you have a partner, they may have noticed it and woken you up. Sleep apnea often causes snoring.

If you have sleep apnea and sleep alone, don't panic. Your body doesn't want you to die while you're sleeping, so your brain gently jolts you out of deep sleep and gets you breathing again.

The problem with this jolting you out of deep sleep over and over is that even if get eight hours of sleep, you don't go through all of the REM and NREM cycles you need for deep, restful sleep. That's why you're sleepy the next day.

Sleep apnea can also cause an increase in LDL blood cholesterol (the "bad" cholesterol), increasing your risk for heart disease. One treatment for sleep apnea is to get a CPAP machine, which is a mask attached to an oxygen machine that helps you continue to breathe. That might sound too weird, but lots of people are doing it these days. It's a thing now.

Not only will it help your reduce the dangerous effects of sleep apnea (including snoring), but sleep apnea diagnosis, treatment and CPAP equipment might be covered by your health insurance.

In addition to sleep apnea, you might have another sleep disorder if you're having problems sleeping and you are eating right, exercising, are in bed for eight hours each night and don't have other habits that would obviously lead to sleep deprivation.

Contact your health care providers and ask for a sleep specialist to determine if you have a sleep disorder.

Sleep Aids

The jury is out regarding just what medications you should take for sleep, how often you should take them and in what doses. Your situation may be due to stress, a time change or other conditions. One sleeping pill won't cure all sleep problems all the time. If you feel you need to take a sleep aid, talk to your doctor to determine what is best for you.

Mattresses

You have many choices for mattresses, including hard, soft, water, self-molding, foam and coiled. Depending on whether you have any spinal or muscle problems, the best mattress for you may come down to simple preference. For most people, a firmer mattress is the best choice because it supports your spine better.

Always test a mattress before you buy. If you like a mattress at a particular hotel you visit, make a note of it. Be careful about falling in love with a mattress after one night's sleep. Your good sleep may have been the result of a variety of factors, including the amount of light in the room, exercise you performed earlier that day, lack of stress, the room temperature, lack of nearby noise, etc.

When was the last time you flipped your mattress? It's a good idea to flip and rotate your mattress every three months, similar to rotating your car tires.

Mark one or all four corners or your mattress so you don't simply turn the mattress back and forth each time. If you don't flip your mattress, you'll end up sleeping with your head at one end and your feet on the other for the life of your mattress. If you want it to wear evenly, flip it the first time, then flip and turn it the second time, and so on, so that you sleep on all four areas of the bed.

The mattress industry recommends changing mattresses every eight years.

Pillows

Your pillows support your neck and head while you sleep. After a time, they lose their ability to adequately support you. If you need to punch your pillow before you go to sleep each night to fluff it up, you probably need to buy a new one.

If you sleep on your side, considers a thicker or firmer pillow to give you the support you need. If you sleep on your back or stomach, you may need less support.

When was the last time you washed your pillowcases and pillows? Pillows absorb the oil, sweat, snot, earwax and drool that leave your body at night. This attracts dust mites that can cause respiratory and allergy problems. If you have a large enough freezer, put your pillows inside for 12 hours to kill mites.

Try White Noise

White noise consists of a sound or sounds you hear that, after a short time, you don't really notice. For example, waves on a beach or steady rain without thunder or lightning are background sounds you get used to and they don't disturb your sleep.

In fact, they can cover other noises that might disturb your sleep, such as traffic or a barking dog outside. Buying a CD of white noise and playing it to get you to sleep may be an effective tool to help you fall asleep quicker, especially when you are in unfamiliar settings, such as a hotel or friend's or family member's home.

Some people sleep with the TV on as white noise. The light can adversely affect your sleep, so cover the screen or find out how to eliminate the picture. An older, larger TV can also raise the temperature in your room.

Another problem with having a TV on while you sleep is that while you may not consciously pay attention to what is coming from the TV, in your sleep state, the programming coming from the TV may affect your dreams. We often try to work out life problems in our dreams. Even if the TV content in your room isn't negative, you may dream about sports, exercise or cooking rather than working out life situations you might otherwise contemplate if you weren't distracted by what's on your TV.

Take a Break Before Bed

Don't go straight from your paperwork or computer to your bed and think you will get the same number of hours and quality of sleep. If your mind is racing after hours of problem-solving or difficult analytical tasks, you will not likely be able to quickly shut these thoughts off.

It's best to knock off work at least 30 minutes before you go to bed if you want to fall asleep faster. If you're going to watch some TV before you go to bed, avoid stressful programs such as horror movies, the nightly news or anything featuring Gordon Ramsey.

If you need to pack a suitcase, wash the dishes or do some other mundane task before you go to bed, save those tasks for after you are done working to give your mind a mental break before you hit the sack.

Food and Sleep

There are no miracle foods that help you sleep. A popular myth promotes eating turkey because it contains tryptophan, which helps get serotonin to the brain. There is not enough tryptophan in foods to have enough of an effect on your sleep.

The real reason you fall asleep after Thanksgiving dinner has more to do with all the complex carbs you eat.

When you eat a big meal, you may feel sleepy afterwards, but that's not because your body is slowing down. In actuality, your metabolism speeds up after you eat. Your circulatory system needs to move more blood, your stomach and pancreas secrete more gastric acid and digestive enzymes and your heart rate rises.

However, you may feel sleepy after a meal because your body has produced more serotonin in response to the carbohydrates you ate. Serotonin, like melatonin, helps you relax and sleep.

While carbohydrates don't have the same effect as a sleeping pill, they are better choices before a nap or night's sleep than protein or fat because they help get more serotonin to your brain. Surprisingly, serotonin plays a role in both triggering sleep and wakefulness.

While you shouldn't look for foods to put you to sleep, you should avoid those that contain caffeine and sugar.

Does what you eat and when you eat it affect your ability to sleep? In short, yes. If you work late and eat when you get home, you may go to bed within an hour or two of your meal. The digestive process and hormonal releases can make it more difficult to fall asleep and get into a deep restful sleep.

There are a variety of myths concerning eating late at night, most having to do with weight gain and fat storage. In a nutshell, the main problem with eating late at night or eating just before sleeping is that it can make restful sleep more difficult.

As far as weight gain and fat storage are concerned, it's how many total calories you eat during the day that is the key factor in weight gain. After that, how physically active you are determines how many calories you will burn. When you eat, then go to sleep, your sleep metabolism will affect your digestive process, but not how your body converts and processes calories.

Caffeine in coffee, tea, sugary drinks, chocolate and spicy foods interfere with sleep. If you drink coffee, tea or energy drinks to help keep you awake during late working hours, think what that will do to you when you finally knock off for work and head to bed.

Avoid alcohol if you need to get a good night's sleep. While alcohol is a depressant, you'll get less restful sleep when the effects on your central nervous system wear off.

Remember this guideline: Eat breakfast like a king, lunch like a prince and dinner like a pauper.

Try to eat no later least three hours before going to sleep. Eat more non-starchy complex carbohydrates, whole grains and nuts, and less fat and protein. It's OK to eat some lean protein with your meal, but look for low-fat choices. Avoid sugar and caffeine. If you want dessert, stick with fruit, rather than baked goods or chocolate.

Drinks like warm milk and non-caffeinated peppermint herb tea may help you get to sleep by relaxing you, but don't affect your physiology and therefore won't work like a drug to help you sleep. Add cocoa or chocolate to milk and you may have even more trouble falling to sleep because of the added caffeine, sugar and theobromine. Some experts recommend cocoa because of its magnesium content. Try a cup of cocoa once or twice before going to bed on a Friday or Saturday night to see how it affects you, rather than when you need a good night's sleep before an important upcoming day.

Exercise and Sleep

Many of us have "slept like a baby" after playing tennis, volleyball, basketball, working hard in the yard, running or exercising.

While the jury is still out on the exact physiological reasons why exercise helps us sleep better, multiple studies on people suffering from insomnia have found that when they exercise, these people sleep better without medication.

What kind of exercise should you do to help yourself get a good night's sleep and when should you do it? Moderately intense activity, such as aerobic exercise that makes you sweat, and performed three hours or more before you want to sleep, may be your best option.

You may be surprised to hear aerobic exercise described as moderate intensity, but this differs from high-intensity exercise such as sprint training. Aerobic exercise uses your slow-twitch muscles fibers and is performed at a rate you can continue for long periods without having to stop.

Sprint or HIIT training takes place at close to your maximum heart rate and you perform sprints in cycles of 30 to 90 seconds, using more high-twitch muscle fibers. Tennis is a good example of an anaerobic activity. Basketball, volleyball, football, racquetball and soccer are other examples. Very high intensity exercise can affect your dopamine levels, interfering with sleep.

It may be that your body's attempt to recover from this physical stress, and specifically lowering your body's temperature, is what causes you to fall asleep more quickly and get a more deep, restful sleep.

One important aspect of exercise recovery may be the temperature affect on your body. You may find it difficult to sleep if you go to bed shortly after exercise because of adrenaline and an elevated body temperature. If you exercise two or three hours before you go to bed, your body temperature, which begins decreasing shortly after you stop exercising, may be able to lower itself better near bedtime, helping you fall asleep quicker.

Keep an exercise and sleep journal to see what type of exercise at what time helps or hinders your sleep.

Chapter Summary

- Sleep is the time when you repair the damage you do to your body during the day.

- Inadequate sleep decreases your body's ability to repair itself and leads to more damage.

- You can't "bank" sleep on weekends or undo the damage done by sleep deprivation during a project or several years.

- Sleep in a dark room. Wake in a room with light.

- Get 8 hours of sleep per night.

- Take naps when you don't get 8 hours.

- Regulate the room temperature

- Try white noise.

- Wear socks to sleep.

- Take a mental break before going to bed.

- No TV in bed – sleep and sex only.

- Exercise three or more hours before bedtime.

- Avoid caffeine; eat eat light carbs closer to bedtime.

- Invest in the right mattress and pillows for you.

- Stay properly hydrated.

- Maintain the same sleep schedule (bedtime and wakeup time) on the weekends that you keep during the week.

Chapter 2: Eating to Enhance Workplace Productivity

Most of the wellness advice you hear and read regarding nutrition focuses on keeping you healthy or helping you lose weight.

That's not the same as eating for workplace performance.

We all know that you should start your day with a good breakfast if you want to perform better at school or work. We also know that healthy eating can help you manage your weight and help reduce your risk for a wide variety of diseases and conditions.

But why do certain foods help you perform better, what combinations of foods are best to eat for improved performance and when you should eat?

Eating for performance focuses on maintaining optimal brain function and energy levels throughout the workday. Even if you're in perfect shape and at the perfect weight, what you eat and when you eat it is important if you want to perform at your peak each day.

The Food and Mood Connection

Your eating habits determine whether you will be alert, sluggish, happy, irritable, focused or groggy. Food fuels your muscles and brain and affects the hormones that regulate bodily functions and emotions.

There is a food and mood connection that's directly tied to how your brain chemistry reacts to certain foods. What you eat affects the production of hormones and neurotransmitters that raise and lower your metabolism and affect your brain function.

Carbohydrates, for example, help produce serotonin, which can make you feel relaxed and pleasant. Too many carbs can make you sleepy and sluggish. Too few can make you tense, nervous and agitated. Chocolate releases endorphins, which are chemicals that block pain and stimulate pleasure. Some types of chocolate contain enough caffeine to stimulate or over stimulate you, depending on what else you've eaten that day. Protein stimulates neurotransmitters that promote alertness.

The key to eating for your workday is to regulate the amount and types of food going into your body so you can keep your blood glucose and insulin levels steady and efficient. This means that you'll want to snack during the day in addition to your regular meals.

How your Body Works

You move your body and you access your brain.

When you move your body, you need to move your muscles. In order to move your muscles and use your brain, you need fuel.

Protein is not a fuel. Protein is a body repair and growth nutrient. It can be a source of fuel if you've depleted your carb stores, but it's harder to metabolize into fuel, and this stresses your body more.

So, what are the fuels for your muscles?

Glycogen (how your body stores carbohydrates) and fat.

How your Brain Works
You've probably all heard that children who eat a good breakfast have better test scores and course grades than kids who don't. Why is that?

Your brain needs glucose (another way your body stores carbs) and oxygen to function.

Glucose is your brain's fuel, so if you keep your brain fueled, it will "run" better.

If you're trying to lose weight by skipping breakfast, your brain doesn't get the glucose it needs and you won't think as well.

For example, an attorney who has skipped breakfast and who is reading pages and pages of opposing counsel's briefs might miss a weakness in her opponent's argument or make error in her own work. The attorney might not be as creative and will come up with fewer ideas to make her case.

- Your brain is roughly 75% water.
- Your (non-water) brain matter is roughly 60% fat.
- Your brain makes up about 2% of your body weight.
- Your brain uses about 20% - 30% of your calories.
- Glucose (a sugar) is the main fuel source for your brain.

In a starvation scenario, your body can convert fat and protein to glycogen if you're deprived of carb stores. When you use fat to create glucose, that fuel can have a side effect like alcohol, impairing your decision-making, awareness and judgment. Long-term Atkins diet-stimulated ketosis is chemically similar to starvation and can lead to dehydration, kidney stress, kidney stones and other problems.

A high-protein diet does not mean that most of your calories from protein. Your body can only metabolize about 35 percent of your daily calories from protein. A "high" protein diet consists of mostly fat calories, then protein (usually 30 percent or less), and then a small amount of carbs (10 percent or less).

Protein is still important for workplace performance, however. If we call carbs "Brain Fuel," we can call protein "Brain Food" because it stimulates the production of neurotransmitters that increase alertness.

Benefits of Performance Eating

Performance eating is aimed at increasing your productivity and efficiency. These aims will accompany your other healthy eating goals.

The benefits of <u>healthy</u> eating include reduced risk for:

- Obesity and overweight
- Diabetes
- Heart attack
- Stroke
- High blood pressure
- Hypertension
- Lower back pain
- Osteoporosis

The benefits of <u>performance</u> eating include:

- Better brain function: more creativity, fewer errors
- More alertness
- Higher energy levels
- Better blood sugar regulation
- Better moods (less irritability, anxiety, depression, stress)

Eating for performance helps you make fewer mistakes and lets you work fewer hours with the same or better results.

Eat More Often

If you don't eat between dinner and lunch the next day, you'll go as long as 18 hours without fueling your body and brain.

How does your car perform after you haven't changed the oil after 10,000 miles? Your car will have to try and function on the sludge that's left in your engine.

Wen you skip breakfast, you deprive your brain of the fuel it needs as you begin trying to perform important intellectual tasks. Research shows that depriving yourself of food can decrease cognitive functions such as processing and understanding new information, memory, verbal skills and spatial and visual understanding.

Would you rather pay a lawyer $300 an hour to work on your important case who hadn't eaten in 18 hours, or one who had eaten a healthy breakfast and a healthy morning snack to keep fueled? Which one would be more likely to be alert, have better cognitive function and be less irritable, tense or sluggish?

If you were going in for open-heart surgery, would you want your doctor to operate on you if he hadn't eaten since the night before and had low blood insulin and glucose levels?

Then why would you ask to be paid full price by a client or employer and then work for them on an empty stomach (and half-empty brain)?

If you're skipping breakfast to try and lose weight, you'll actually increase the likelihood you'll gain weight.

You don't overeat when you're not hungry—you overeat when you're "starved." If you stuff yourself with excess calories, your body won't be able to metabolism them and will store them as fat.

Forget the big lunches and late dinners you think are buying you extra hours of work—they actually make you less productive and you will likely only increase the quantity of lower-quality work you do.

Suggested Eating Schedule

A good eating schedule for maintaining workplace productivity would look something like this:

7:00 am – Breakfast
10:00 am – Snack
12:00 pm – Lunch
3:00 pm – Snack
6:00 pm – Dinner

Snack Like You Mean It

The key to controlling calories and maintaining blood glucose levels is to eat at least two healthy snacks during the day. Your snacking needs to be proactive, not reactive. This means you need to plan your snacks each day, rather than simply heading to the vending machine each time you feel peckish.

Snacking for peak performance is not that difficult, even at work. You can keep a number of healthy snacks in your desk drawer, such as granola bars, oatmeal packets, microwave popcorn, trail mix, granola and nuts. If you work from home, keep your refrigerator stocked with sliced carrots and celery, fresh fruit and dips like hummus.

You don't need to fill yourself up with a large snack to regulate your glucose levels throughout the day. A quick, healthy snack at work might be as simple as half a banana and a handful of nuts.

Stay away from the vending machine! Sugary snacks and drinks give you a quick spike in your blood sugar levels, but will make you crash later.

Snacking is important for:

- Maintaining blood sugar levels (energy)
- Fueling the brain
- Preventing cravings (fat and sugar)
- Overeating

Try to eat something every four hours to keep your blood sugar and energy levels stable throughout the day, recommends Page Love, RDN, owner of Nutrifit Sport Therapy in Atlanta.

"Look for a carb/protein combination in snacks, such as fruit and cheese or yogurt and pretzels or a balanced energy bar," recommends Love.

Other good snack combinations include:

- Carton of milk
- Piece of fruit with nuts
- ½ a bagel with cream cheese
- Apple slices with cheese
- Celery with nut butter
- Lightly salted popcorn and jerky
- Trail mix
- Yogurt cup with crackers
- Packet of plain oatmeal with pat of butter or dash of milk
- Veggies with hummus dips
- Crackers and cheese
- Smoothie

Keep snacks around 100 to 200 calories, based on your weight.

When to Eat Carbs, Proteins and Fats

You'll want to regulate your blood glucose throughout the day and maintain a good mix of carbohydrates, protein and fat.

As we mentioned earlier, having sugar will give you a temporary spike in energy but will cause you to crash even lower than where you started when the sugar spike wears off.

Start your day with a breakfast that consists of roughly two-thirds complex carbohydrates and one-third lean protein. Your mid-morning snack, lunch and/or afternoon snack can include more protein if they come from lean sources, but should still be about 50/50 carbs and protein.

If you are going to eat one meal that is protein-heavy, such as one with beef, pork or chicken as the "main" dish, make that meal lunch. You'll have plenty of time to digest that meal before you go to bed in the evening.

If you want meat for dinner, add it to a stir-fry or pasta, rather than having a large piece of meat with one or two sides. The fat from your protein will get all over the rice, pasta or veggies, giving you that flavor you crave with every forkful, but with much less fat and fewer calories.

Complex carbohydrates, as opposed to simple sugars, include foods such as vegetables, rice, pasta, potatoes and breads. Concentrate on whole grain pastas and breads, brown rice, sweet potatoes and other "non-white," "non-starchy" or low-glycemic carbs. In the appendix of this books is a list of healthy carb choices.

If you are eating later in the evening, eat more carbs and less protein to avoid eating that interferes with your sleep. Have more of your daily protein at lunch, such as fish or chicken or turkey breast meat, rather than trying to down a steak at night.

Getting Boosts From Stimulants Isn't Smart
Avoid stimulants like coffee and energy shots. They are not a good substitute for glucose and protein.

A cup of coffee as your breakfast is false stimulant energy that only lasts about an hour, says Love. Because of the crash after a stimulant wears off, you'll end up with a negative energy balance later in the day.

As far as energy shots that promise no crash, that's misleading. Their contention is that after the energy boost from the shot wears off, you'll go back to your previous, normal metabolic state. That's still a crash from your shot "high" back down to your "normal" state.

If you want to try an energy boost drink, experiment with it on the weekend, not when you are under the gun and need energy during your workweek. Imagine what a worse predicament you'll be in if you rely on one of these shots to keep you going and it doesn't help, or if you do crash at some point after taking it.

Tips for Performance Eating
The key to performance eating is to keep your metabolism fueled throughout the day, eating the right mix of carbs, fat and protein approximately every four hours.

For an optimal performance diet (which can mirror a weight-management diet), eat breakfast like a king, lunch like a prince and dinner like a pauper, with a mid-morning snack and a mid-afternoon snack.

Your carbs and protein should be a ratio of approximately 2/3 carbs to 1/3 protein for the day, and at each meal, if possible, to maintain energy levels and alertness.

Junk carbs, which are high in sugar, can give you a short-term energy spike, but within an hour or so, you'll crash. High-glycemic, sugary foods include pastries, white potatoes, soda, some fruits, white rice, white bread and many processed cereals. Pasta is actually not a high-glycemic food because of how your body's digestive process processes it.

Opt for fruits and vegetables that make up the colors of the rainbow.

Fats don't burn as quickly as carbs, so they satisfy your appetite better and help you stay full longer. Include healthy fats to avoid sugar cravings and to keep you full longer. Your caloric intake of healthy fat for the day can be more than your intake of protein.

Dining Out

Most businesspeople will not be able to avoid dining out. You may also feel it's necessary at times to stop at the drive-through of fast food restaurants and eat in the card to accommodate your busy schedule.

Just because you can't eat healthy doesn't mean you can't eat healthier.

For example, if you order a Burger King Whopper without the cheese and mayo, you'll reduce the fat by almost 50 percent and the calories by almost 30 percent, according to the nutrition information at Burger King's website.

Compare a serving of a Domino's pizza with sausage and pepperoni to a serving with mushrooms, onions and green peppers. The veggie pizza has approximately 35 percent less fat, 20 percent fewer calories and 30 percent less sodium.

So, while a hamburger or pizza may not be anyone's definition of health food, a burger without the mayo and cheese and a veggie pizza are healthier fast-food options if you can't give up your favorites.

Keeping this type of food substitution in mind, you can begin to shift your eating to even healthier options without giving up comfort foods or subsisting on tofu and sprouts.

For example, skip the hamburger in spaghetti sauce and order tomato instead of Alfredo sauce. Order a vegetable soup instead of a cream-based one. Have a bean burrito with salsa and avocado instead of one with ground beef, cheese and sour cream.

You can also order dishes that aren't on the menu. Even during busy times, kitchens may at least modify menu items. For example, ask for crushed nuts or a sprinkle of sesame seeds on your salad instead of croutons. Ask to hold the mayo and cheese on a burger and for extra tomatoes and lettuce. When you order French onion soup, ask for no crouton or cheese. Skip the cheese and sour cream that comes with chili. Ask for salsa with a baked potato instead of sour cream, cheese and bacon. Try fajitas with back beans instead of steak or chicken.

Another thing to keep in mind is that many restaurants put all their orders into a computer—the server might not be able to enter a completely new dish you order, even if the chef could make it. Ask for a simple substitution a busy chef can make when you consider your dining options.

Ignore Mom

How many times did your mother tell you, "Don't eat that, you'll spoil your dinner!"?

Ignore mom and help control your calories. If you are going out to eat with co-workers or clients, have a small snack before you leave the office. By the time you get to the restaurant, you will be less likely to be "starving" to the point you order an appetizer or want to super size your order.

Start with a cup of soup or side salad before you eat your main entrée and you'll be able to order a smaller entree and still be full. In fact, you may be able to fill yourself with a cup of soup, small salad, piece of whole grain bread and glass of tea, juice or water.

If you're going to a business reception or cocktail party where hors d' oeuvre will be served, snack before you get there so you can control yourself once the food appears. These functions often occur in the evening before dinner, and if you haven't eaten since lunch, you may make these high-calorie, high-fat snacks your dinner. If you're going out to dinner after a reception, this can make things even worse.

Fast-Food Tips

- Hold the mayo and cheese on hamburgers and other sandwiches. Add more lettuce and tomatoes for extra moisture.

- Order grilled chicken sandwiches instead of fried.

- Skip the meat on pizza.

- Order thin-crust pizza.

- Ask for less cheese on your pizza.

- Order a bean burrito. Skip the sour cream and cheese and add salsa.

Sit-Down Restaurant Tips

- Order a glass of water and drink at least half, even if you order soda.

- Start every meal with a cup (not a bowl) of low-fat soup or a salad. Skip the crackers and bread.

- Don't eat more than five chips if you get a basket.

- Have a snack before you go to a sit-down restaurant.

- Order modified versions of menu items.

Performer's Breakfast Items

Oatmeal – Add a dash of skim milk, pat of butter substitute or a few raisins to this slow-digesting, high-fiber Super food.

Cold cereal – Some are made from nuts; choose those higher in complex carbs and lower in sugar.

Breads – Choose whole grain toast, bagels and muffins. Add nut butter or cream cheese for a good carb/protein mix.

Yogurt – Add protein to your carbs with a cup of low-fat yogurt. Mix in pieces of fresh fruit or crunchy granola.

Fruit – Canned or fresh, fruit is a good source of vitamins and minerals and sweetens cereals, oatmeal, waffles and pancakes.

Waffles and pancakes – Choose whole grain versions and use a pat of non-fat butter substitute, a dash of syrup, a bit of yogurt or some fruit for extra flavor.

Cottage cheese – Use the fat-free variety as a small side dish and flavor it with fruit. This is a good source of protein and calcium.

Turkey bacon – If you need some meat, try a low-fat bacon made from turkey breast.

Lean ham – A good meat choice with pancakes and waffles.

Eggs –Dietary cholesterol is not atherogenic, and eggs offer lean protein, vitamins and healthy fat.

Coffee cup "omelet" – Make a quick soufflé with eggs, veggies, lean ham and low-fat cheese. Put the mixture in a coffee cup and heat for 30 seconds. Stir the mixture and cook for another 30-60 seconds to your desired consistency.

Performer's Lunch Items

Low-fat soups – Instead of cream-based soups, choose vegetable varieties like tomato, onion, celery and black bean.

Salads – Order dressing on the side and dip your fork in it before you spear your salad each time. Skip croutons and add nuts and seeds. Skip creamy dressings and cheese. Add a few spoonfuls of cottage cheese.

Sandwiches – Use whole grain bread. Skip mayo or use fat-free mayo or mustard. Use a small amount of lean meat to flavor sandwiches packed with lettuce, tomatoes, onions, sprouts, cucumbers, shaved carrots and avocadoes. Put the meat on the top so your first taste is the meat. Use turkey and chicken breast and lean ham.

Bean burrito – Choose vegetarian or fat-free refried beans and add shredded lettuce, tomatoes, onions, avocado, salsa and low-fat sour cream. Serve with Spanish rice with diced red and green peppers.

Tuna and chicken salad – Use low-fat or fat-free mayo. Use chicken breast meat or water-packed "light" canned tuna. Season with curry powder or tarragon. Add celery and onions, slivered almonds for crunch and grapes for sweetness.

Ground turkey sliders – If you haven't tried ground turkey burgers, you'll be hooked once you do. Order one or two turkey sliders made with breast meat instead of a quarter pound beef burger to reduce calories and fat. Pile on the lettuce, tomato and onions. Serve with a side like baked sweet potato fries, low-fat potato salad or baked beans.

Performer's Dinner Items

Pasta – Choose whole-grain pasta and don't drown it in sauce. Choose tomato sauce or toss it lightly in olive oil and garlic. Flavor with shrimp, chicken breast strips or canned tuna.

Salmon – Bake, poach, grill or broil. Season with black pepper or garam masala. Bake or broil over asparagus spears, mushrooms and thin slices of potato.

Pizza – Choose a whole-grain, thin crust. Top with half the normal amount of cheese. Add your favorite veggies.

Chicken breast – Grill, bake or broil. Season lightly with salt and pepper, tarragon or garam masala. Serve with a half a sweet potato and mixed vegetables.

Beef – The closer you are to bedtime, the less beef you should eat. Choose leaner cuts of beef, such as sirloin or flank. They're less expensive and have less and fat. Use beef to flavor stir-fry dishes, rather than having a large piece of meat with several side dishes. Serve with baked beans and fresh vegetables.

Mac and cheese – Use whole-grain pasta, low-fat cheese and skim milk for this dish. Skip the eggs, butter and full cheese and add tarragon to your low-fat cheese sauce for an upscale, grownup comfort food. Add sliced cherry tomatoes and a small amount of lean ham cubes. Add sliced onions or mushrooms for a more savory flavor. Serve with a salad and fat-free dressing.

Breakfast for Dinner – No one says you can't have a couple of pancakes or waffles and a slice of lean ham for dinner. Serve with a pat of non-fat butter substitute, a dash of syrup and fresh fruit. Avoid orange, grapefruit or tomato juice if the acid will keep you awake later.

How Much Water?

Staying hydrated is important because many people mistake thirst for hunger and end up eating calories they don't need. Because you get most of the water you need from the foods you eat and drinks you have with your meals, a glass or bottle of water between breakfast and lunch, and a drink in the afternoon should be all you need to stay properly hydrated.

If you eat mostly processed foods, this can lead to dehydration. Follow your thirst as a guide to how much water you need each day.

One way to make sure you keep snacking and drinking for performance is to set an alarm on your computer or watch or fitness wearable that reminds you in the mid-morning and mid-afternoon to take a snack/drink break.

It's also a myth that you shouldn't drink water shortly before, during or after meals because it dilutes the enzymes responsible for digestion. This isn't true; water helps break down food and can make it easier to digest.

If you drink a glass of water before a meal, you may also eat fewer calories. Don't artificially decrease your calorie intake by filling yourself with water as a diet strategy—drink water before meals only as a way to help you refrain from overeating.

If drinking water before a meal helps prevent you from going back for seconds, that's a good strategy. If drinking more than one glass of water fills you to the point that you can get away with having an energy bar for lunch, that's not a good idea.

Remember, water will not stay in your stomach, keeping you full, until your next meal. You'll pass that water and be hungry again soon, leading to poor snacking or a reliance on the dreaded "willpower" to ignore hunger pangs until your next meal.

The Low-Carb Myth

Think of yourself as if you are an automobile. You are made primarily of steel and use either gasoline or diesel as fuel. Just because you're made of steel doesn't mean you run on steel. Shoving steel in your gas tank to try and make yourself go isn't too bright.

After water, your biggest body components are fat and protein with less than 1 percent of you made up of carbohydrates.

So, even though much of your body is made from protein, your body runs on glycogen and fat. How much of each depends on whether you're doing aerobic or anaerobic activity.

Just as you wouldn't stuff steel down your car's gas tank, you don't want to stuff your body with protein if you want to make yourself run. When you are at the office, your main fuel should be complex carbohydrates.

It took the mainstream media decades to finally understand the obvious fallacy of high-protein, low-carb diets, which credible dietitians knew to dismiss from the beginning of the fad.

Because of the amount of advertising purchased by proponents of low-carb diets and fantastic claims made by these marketers, the media basically ignored the fact no research proved that low-carb diets reduced weight (long-term) more than "mainstream" diets. The media also didn't look into the fact that these fad diets caused problems such as dehydration, kidney problems, lack of calcium and other issues.

For peak performance, eat a diet that's 50 percent to 60 percent complex carbohydrates, with the rest of your calories coming from healthy fats, then protein.

The Skinny on Fat

Credible nutrition experts now recommend that we eat more fat than what's been recommended in previous decades. This is because not all fats are unhealthy and a meal with fat satisfies your hunger better than a meal that's primarily carbohydrates, which burn quicker and can cause you to be hungry sooner.

If you eat healthy fats, such as those found in plants and fish, you can eat more fat. Examples of foods rich in healthy monounsaturated and polyunsaturated fat and omega-3 fatty acids include olive oil, peanut butter and salmon.

Saturated and trans fats, found in large quantities in animal products and processed foods, such as baked goods, are the ones you want to avoid. Trans fats are so bad for you, the U.S. Food and Drug Administration banned them from commercial foods as of June 18, 2018.

Cutting down on "bad" carbs or "white" carbs lets you eat more complex carbohydrates with more benefits. For example, instead of a white potato, eat a sweet potato. Instead of white bread, eat whole grain bread. Eat more veggies than sugary carbs. Because of the way it's digested, pasta is actually not a sugary carb.

When you eat protein, choose lean sources. Coldwater fish, such as salmon and tuna, chicken and turkey breast meat, nuts, eggs, beans, peas and low-fat dairy products are good choices of lean protein.

Don't Panic About Dietary Cholesterol

Most of the cholesterol in your blood is manufactured by your liver, along with a few other glands and organs. The cholesterol you get from food (dietary cholesterol) does not get into your arteries, harden and increase your risk of heart attack.

Trying to avoid dietary cholesterol can lead to food substitutions that increase your intake of sugar (e.g., waffles and pancakes instead of bacon and eggs), which stimulates the production of LDL particles that carry LDL cholesterol (the "bad" cholesterol) into your arteries.

The fact that sugar, not dietary cholesterol, increases your risk for heart disease, doesn't mean you should opt for a low-carb, high-protein diet. This simply means that you shouldn't overeat sugar.

Eating a balanced diet of healthy carbs, healthy fats and lean protein, and getting regular exercise reduces your risk of heart disease.

Eating lots of protein and getting inadequate vitamins and minerals (due to a lack of fruits and vegetables) will lead to a host of other health problems.

Eating Slower Reduces Calorie Intake

Have you ever eaten a plate of food, decided to go back for seconds, then been interrupted with a phone call or e-mail? Did you notice that after you hung up the phone or hit "send," you weren't hungry any more and didn't have that second helping?

One reason why people gain weight is because they overeat, based on how fast they eat. It takes approximately 15 minutes for the hormones that tell your brain your stomach is full to make it from your stomach to your brain.

This is why it's almost impossible to take only one plate at a buffet. You've finished your first plate, which may probably included a huge amount of calories, but you're still hungry since you ate it in less than 15 minutes. You smell all this wonderful food sitting just a few feet away and go back for seconds.

Quite often, people who go to buffets can't finish the second plate of food they've taken because their brain finally "catches up" to their stomach while they are eating that plateful of food. Or, after you finish the second plate, you are extremely uncomfortable, or stuffed, all at once with no warning.

If you work from home, you may eat a plate of food that has more than enough calories to satisfy you, but during those minutes of lag time between your stomach and brain talking to each other, you head back to the kitchen for seconds.

You might also eat a frozen dinner or small portion at lunch and feel less than satisfied at the table. However, if you can wait 15 minutes, by the time you get back to the office, you are often satiated without eating anything else.

Realizing that hunger pangs at the lunch or dinner table are only temporary and that you won't feel this hunger for long will help you reduce the temptation to have seconds or order dessert.

If you eat slower, your stomach will "catch up" to your brain and you'll be less likely to have seconds. This doesn't necessarily mean chewing more or taking longer between forkfuls. Penn State researchers found that people who ate a bowl of soup to start their meal ended up eating 20 percent fewer calories each time.

How Many Calories?

How many calories you should eat each day depends on your age, height, weight and activity levels. There are many free, online calorie calculators to help you dtermine the right number for you.

Below is a chart that lists the U.S. Department of Agriculture daily calorie recommendations based on the 2015-2020 Dietary Guidelines for Americans.

USDA Daily Recommended Calories

Women

Age	Sedentary	Moderately Active	Active
19-25	2,000	2,200	2,400
26-30	1,800	2,000	2,400
31-50	1,800	2,000	2,200
51-60	1,600	1,800	2,200
61+	1,600	1,800	2,000

Men

Age	Sedentary	Moderately Active	Active
Age	Sedentary	Moderately Active	Active
19-20	2,600	2,800	3,000
21-25	2,400	2,800	3,000
26-35	2,400	2,600	3,000
36-40	2,400	2,600	2,800
41-45	2,200	2,600	2,800
46-55	2,200	2,400	2,800
56-65	2,200	2,400	2,600
66-75	2,000	2,200	2,600
76+	2,000	2,200	2,400

Height & Weight - This chart uses an example woman who is 5'4" and 126 lbs., and an example man who is 5'10" and 154 lbs.

Activity Level - "Active" means your daily routine includes physical activity similar to walking more than 3 miles at 3 to 4 mph. "Moderately Active" means your daily routine includes activity similar to walking 1.5 to 3 miles at 3 to 4 mph. "Sedentary" means you do little physical activity other than the ordinary tasks associated with daily living.

Chapter Summary

- Performance eating is different from weight management/heart health eating.

- Performance eating focuses on regulating your metabolism and brain function.

- Carbohydrates, not protein, should be your main source of fuel.

- Eating some protein helps promote alertness.

- Eating more healthy fats decreases cravings and reduces overeating.

- Skipping breakfast is really stupid.

- Eat at least five times each day (three meals each day and two snacks).

- Keep meals around 400-600 calories and snacks to 100-200 calories.

- Drink a glass of water each morning and afternoon.

- Eat more protein earlier in the day and less later.

- Avoid energy drinks.

- Trying to avoid dietary cholesterol can result in unhealthy substitutes.

Chapter 3: Maintaining your Energy Levels in the Workplace

Most corporate wellness programs address general health and fitness, which includes long-term diet and exercise programs.

That's obviously important for reducing corporate fatigue; however, high-performing, high-stress workers want to focus on helpful workplace physical activity and off-site exercise that emphasizes strengthening and recovery rather than just weight loss and heart health.

Physical fitness is important for promoting general long-term health for a wide variety of reasons. It can help reduce your risk for a wide variety of diseases and conditions.

- Heart disease
- Stroke
- High blood pressure
- Hypertension
- Type II diabetes
- Chronic back pain

Exercise also provides a wide variety of health and fitness benefits that can keep you on the job and decrease tardiness, absenteeism and sick days. This, in turn, reduces health care costs and increases productivity. Benefits of exercise include:

- Improved mental acuity
- Improved sleep
- Reduced lower back pain
- Improved heart health
- Weight loss and maintenance
- Reduced stress
- Improved blood cholesterol
- Reduced risk of heart attack and stroke

We know that for businesses, employees who are physically fit benefit the company in a variety of ways over the long-term:

- Improved productivity
- Improved efficiency
- Less absenteeism
- Less presenteeism
- Lower health care costs
- Higher employee retention
- Fewer workers' comp claims
- Fewer lawsuits

When it comes to daily peak performance and reducing corporate fatigue, you should also try to manage your every day energy levels.

The <u>outcome</u> goals for energy management should include:

- Alertness
- Creativity
- Problem-solving ability
- Avoiding mental fatigue and errors
- Boosting work product quality

The <u>process</u> goals for energy management should include:

- Keeping blood sugar levels more even
- Maintaining optimal metabolism rates
- Promoting good blood circulation
- Promoting good cardiorespiratory function (oxygen to the brain)
- Muscle strengthening
- Muscle nourishment

Don't Sweat it

It seems that every month, we're seeing a new study that shows people who sit during the day for work have <u>much</u> higher mortality rates than people who don't have desk jobs.

You will improve your productivity if you are able to get more oxygen to your brain during the day, maintain a healthy resting heart rate, have good blood circulation, release chemicals that improve your mood, and generally keep your metabolism up during the day.

You don't need to lift weights, go jogging, work out in a gym or use an exercise machine to stay active in the workplace—you can maintain an adequate metabolism level for good workplace productivity with a few simple techniques in your office and around the workplace.

Yes, vigorous exercise is extremely helpful for long-term weight loss and general health, but if you aren't interested in or can't commit to a regular exercise program, you can still perform a variety of simple activities each day that will raise your metabolism throughout your workday, improving your brain function—all without causing you to break a sweat.

Even if you are into exercise and are in great shape, your metabolism can still go down to unproductive levels during the day and you should try to get physical in and around the office to increase your heart rate, blood circulation and metabolism during working hours.

Create Peaks and Valleys Throughout the Day

Sitting at your desk from 8:00 am and not moving until lunch is not a good idea. Raising your heart rate every 30, 60 or 90 minutes will help you perform better because of the increased oxygen flow to your brain and blood circulation throughout your body.

Taking a few minutes to raise your metabolism will prevent your heart rate from settling into a very low number of beats per minute. Just as raising your heart rate too high is bad for your health, letting your heart rate drop very low and stay there is bad for your productivity.

Getting up from your desk, walking around the office, doing a few quick exercises or walking up and down a flight of stairs or two is all you need to raise your metabolism for improved productivity.

And you don't need to break a sweat.

Physical Activity In the Workplace vs. Exercise

Exercise requires more of a mental, physical and time commitment than high-performing employees can give during the day and most evenings.

Physical activity, such as walking stairs, doesn't require those three commitments. Even moderately intense (vs. vigorous) activity can improve workplace performance:

- Increased metabolism
- More oxygen to the brain
- Improved cognitive function
- Release of norepinephrine
- Decreased errors
- More productivity (get your work done sooner)
- Increased alertness
- Increased alertness

Managing your Metabolism While Working

Add a "stress alarm" to your day. Use your watch, computer or smartphone to ping you every 90 minutes or so to remind you to get up from your desk if you haven't yet.

Or, you can set a mid-morning and mid-morning afternoon ping to remind you to go walk up and down stairs for five minutes to get some more oxygen to your brain, elevate your heart rate and keep you energy levels going. You can combine these breaks with taking your snacks.

For one week, wear a heart rate monitor to see if your heart rate gets too low throughout the day. This will let you know if you're too sedentary.

What should your heart rate be? One weekend morning when you're not in a hurry or stressed, find your heart rate after you wakeup. This will be your resting heart rate. Keeping your heart rate slightly higher than your resting heart rate will keep your energy levels up.

Check your resting heart rate each month. If it's going up, that can be a sign of heart problems in the future. Typical resting heart rates for non-athletes are 60 to 90 beats per minute. Athletes have lower heart rates, a slow as the low 30s.

Stop eating lunch at your desk for one week. Note how you feel at the end of that week as opposed to the week before, when you at lunch at your desk.

"But I can get two or three more hours of work done per week if I eat at my desk! That comes to 100 to 150 more hours of work per year!"

No it doesn't. Work fills time. The more time you have available, the slower you'll work and more breaks you'll take (especially on the internet).

Use a pedometer to track workday steps. Use that data to increase your steps each day.

Arrive early the airport (to reduce stress) and avoid working while waiting at the gate. Take a walk.

Try micro workouts (5 – 10 minutes) of light calisthenics that raise your heart rate and increase breathing.

Ask your employer for an onsite workout room. The company won't need to provide any cardio equipment, just space for calisthenics and maybe some mats, steps and resistance bands.

Try a standing or walking desk.

Take Advantage of Stairs

How hard is it to walk up one or two flights of stairs? Stairs are an excellent fitness tool for breaks. Here's a good pattern for using stairs to raise your metabolism each day:

- Get off the elevator two flights early when you come to work in the morning and walk the last two floors.

- After you've been at your desk for 90 minutes or so, leave your office and walk up and down two flights of stairs. You can also do this after your mid-morning snack break.

- When you leave for lunch, take two flights of stairs down and get on the elevator on that floor.

- Get off the elevator two flights early when you return from lunch.

- Walk up and down two flights of stairs at least once during the afternoon.

- When you leave work, get off the elevator two floors early, or take the stairs down two floors before you get on the elevator.

This simple pattern will result in your walking up and down 16 flights of stairs each day, 80 flights each week, and 320 to 400 flights of stairs each month. During a 50-week work year, you'll walk 4,000 flights of stairs.

When you walk up stairs, you use more calf muscle to lift your body's weight and propel you upward. When you walk down stairs, you engage the quads more to brake you, varying your muscle use.

Depending on your office or your physical condition, you may only need to walk up and down one flight of stairs to get a quick heart rate increase, or you may need to walk more than two flights.

Using stairs to elevate your heart rate, improve your circulation and get more oxygen to your brain is a simple, effective way to increase your productivity on the job.

Desk Exercises

Performing two or more minutes of simple movements in your chair or in front of your desk will help you get a quick burst of energy and raise your metabolism.

Hip and Butt Raises—Place your feet together in front of you. Place your hands on your chair near your hips. Raise your self slightly off your chair (you don't need to stand up straight) and lower yourself, repeating this exercise for 30 to 60 seconds.

Try this same exercise with your legs off the floor, straight in front of you. Use your arms to raise your butt slightly off the chair.

Desk Pushups—Stand in front of your desk and lean forward, placing your hands on your desk. Use your arms to raise and lower yourself, performing these pushups for 30 to 60 seconds.

Ups and Downs—Stand in front of your desk with your feet about shoulder width and your hands on your hips. Bend forward and touch your hands to your knees, then touch your toes. Raise up and put your hands back on your hips, then reach as high toward the ceiling as possible. Repeat this pattern for 60 seconds.

More Serious Exercise

If you would like to improve your heart health, lose some weight, improve your sleep, better deal with stress and help avoid diseases and conditions such as high blood pressure, heart attack and stroke, you don't have to perform grueling, stressing, boring or unenjoyable workouts that cause you pain and leave you stiff and sore the next day.

The key to starting an exercise program is finding an activity or activities you enjoy doing. Choosing a piece of exercise equipment or signing up for a gym membership only because you know that it will be effective in getting you in shape or helping you lose weight is not a smart idea. If you don't look forward to your fitness activity, you'll start skipping workouts and eventually may quit altogether.

Enjoyment (fun!) should be your number one priority when choosing a long-term exercise activity if you want to stick with it. You can turn almost any physical activity into exercise with a few modifications to what you're doing, so think about enjoyable physical activities as you begin your planning.

If you like to play tennis or racquetball, schedule time for those and stick to your playing schedule. If you prefer to work out alone, don't sign up for an exercise class, no matter how good you've heard it is. If you are more social, sign up for a gym membership. If you hate jogging because of the leg and back pain it causes, but don't mind walking, choose that activity.

Exercise Choices

There is no one type of exercise or workout that is best for everyone. You can get the benefits you want by performing a variety of exercises and workout routines, and may even want to cross train with several activities, rather than sticking with one workout each time.

Depending on your goals, you have the following options:

Fat-Burning Workouts

"Fat-burning" is not a scientific term for workouts and generally refers to exercise done at a pace comparable to a brisk walk. When you exercise below your aerobic heart rate, you burn a higher percentage of calories from fat than when you do more intense workouts, which is why some people refer to this as fat-burning exercise. You'll actually burn less fat doing this type of exercise because you burn fewer total fat calories as compared to an aerobic workout. Fat-burning exercise still burns calories and is an excellent way to start building the cardiorespiratory stamina and Muscular endurance you'll need for more intense exercise.

Aerobic Exercise

Aerobic exercise is activity you perform at a heart rate similar to the one you reach when jogging. You should be breathing hard, sweating, but still able to talk. If you can't talk, you're exercising in the anaerobic heart rate range, and may soon fatigue and have to stop.

You can use a heart rate monitor to gauge your aerobic target heart rate, which is 70 percent to 80 percent of your maximum heart rate, but heart rate formulas are often inaccurate. Some heart rate formulas and monitors you wear or that come with machines provide you with a good general guide for your workout intensity; however, you can follow your body's own feelings to achieve the best heart rate for exercise. The key is to find the maximum pace you can continually maintain for 15 minutes or longer without having to take frequent breaks.

Sprint/Interval Training/HIIT

When you have a hard workday, is it more like a steady, moderately intense, evenly paced jog, or a tennis match with waves of ups and downs?

So how should you train your body?

Aerobic exercise helps you burn calories and improve cardiorespiratory function. It does <u>not</u> help you train your ability to recover from stress.

High-intensity interval training (HIIT), which consists of repeated, short bursts of activity followed by slower recovery periods, is better for high-stress workers.

When you go jogging for 30 minutes or an hour, you stress your body the entire time, but you only recover once, when you stop running.

This is the type of cardio exercise most people do on a treadmill, elliptical, glider or rowing machine, or in an aerobics class.

When you do HITT, you stress yourself for 1-2 minutes, then recover for 1 to 2 minutes, depending on your level of fitness.

During each of these short recovery periods, your body works to repair and strengthen itself. This type of exercise is much more beneficial for most people, even those who have a goal of weight loss or weight-management.

High-intensity interval training is performed at 80 percent to 90 percent of your maximum heart rate, or near your maximum effort. Without a heart rate monitor, you should aim for an intensity that almost exhausts you within 90 seconds. You then take a two-minute recovery break and then perform another sprint.

You can do this at a lower intensity with shorter intervals and recovery times.

One method of exercising this way is with circuit training. Circuit training is a method of exercise that moves you from exercise to exercise, performing each one at a high intensity for a very short period of time to raise your hear rate.

For example, if you lift weights to build muscles, like a bodybuilder, you lift the maximum weight you can lift, or close to it. You perform only three to five lifts per set, taking a break after each set.

With circuit training, you perform an exercise using about 50 to 75 percent of your maximum weight or effort for 30 to 60 seconds, depending on what shape you're in. You take only a 15- to 30-second break and then move to a new exercise. You might take a break of several minutes every 10 minutes, but your goal is to keep your heart rate high during the entire course of your workout.

You can use single- or multiple-exercise circuits. For a single-exercise circuit-training workout, you might perform jumping jacks for one minute, take a short break, then move to biceps curls, then do crunches and so on. With a multiple-exercise circuit-training workout, you might do 60 seconds of running in place, immediately move to 60 seconds of situps without a break, then move to another exercise, completing six, 60-second exercises before taking a one-minute break. You then repeat the circuit.

It's important to consult with a fitness professional or your doctor before you try this type of exercise. Even adding a few sprints to aerobic workouts should be OK'd by your doctor before you try it.

Resistance Exercises

Resistance exercise focuses on building muscle. You use weights, resistance bands, exercise machines or bodyweight exercises to slightly damage your muscle fibers. When your muscles recover and repair themselves, they grow larger.

While you may not be interested in bodybuilding, using some resistance during exercise, including during beginner and cardio workouts, can help you increase your calorie burn throughout the day and improve your fitness levels.

Working your core and lower back muscles, for example, can help reduce lower back pain. American workers lose more than 100 million workdays each year due to lower back pain, according to the Wellness Council of America. Larger muscles also burn more calories while you're sitting at your desk or going about your normal daily activities.

Creating a Home Workout Area

If you can dedicate an area in your home for exercise, you'll be more likely to exercise on a regular basis. If you have to drag out a machine or find and set up other equipment, you may skip your workout.

It's easy to create a workout space or room in your home with items you have around the house. If you're more motivated, you can outfit your exercise area with variety of low-cost cardio and resistance equipment.

To begin, find a space in your home you can use each time you want to work out. If you need to use the room or space for other work, you'll just need a small container for any items you want to keep in the room.

Make sure the room is well ventilated, well lit and preferably has a ceiling height that will let you raise your arms and jump slightly. The floor should be level and firm, but not hard. If you have a wood, tile or concrete floor, buy an exercise mat.

Have a table for your cell phone, water bottle, glasses, towel or other items. If you plan on keeping items like resistance bands, a jump rope, dumbbells or an ab wheel in the room, keep a box in the room.

Add some creature comforts, such as a TV you can watch during workouts to make them go faster. If you have a DVD player, you can follow along with workout programs. Leave a radio, iPod or other player in the room if you enjoy music or want to listen to an audio book.

Include some or all of these items to help you work out:

- Dumbbells
- Resistance bands
- Gym ball
- Kettlebell
- Ab wheel
- Jump rope
- Hula hoop
- Plastic milk jugs/soda bottles (water-filled weights)
- Bike trainer/stand
- Chin-up bar
- Two, stable chairs (for dips)
- Heart rate monitor

Target Heart Rates

Your target heart rate range is the number of heartbeats per minute you want to achieve during exercise. You don't need to hit one number, but instead want to be in a range that lets you know whether you are in your fat-burning, aerobic or anaerobic heart rate range.

You target heart rate range for each level of exercise is a percentage of your maximum heart rate, or how many beats your heart can make in one minute.

For beginners, your fat-burning heart rate range is roughly 50 percent to 60 percent of your maximum heart rate. Aerobic exercise takes place at 65 percent to 80 percent of your maximum heart rate. Sprint training takes place at 80 percent to 90 percent of your maximum heart rate.

To calculate your maximum heart rate, you can take a treadmill stress test, administered by a health professional, input data into a heart rate monitor, or use a manual calculation.

For many years, people used the formula 220 minus Your Age to get their maximum heart rate. This was never intended by the physician who offered it as a general example at a health conference, but the public soon began to misquote this formula as the Holy Grail for determining maximum heart rate. This led to women working harder than they thought they were.

There is no universally accepted formula for manually calculating maximum heart rate, but Northwestern Memorial Hospital researchers determined that adult women should subtract 88 percent of their age from 206 to get the most accurate maximum heart rate. Of the many other formulas available, most will give you a maximum heart rate within two or three beats of each other.

Using the Northwestern formula, a 30-year-old formula would multiply 30 X .88 to get 26.4. She would subtract that from 206 to get 179.6. To get her target heart rate range for exercise, she would multiply 179.6 by .70 and .80 to get a target heart rate range for aerobic exercise of roughly 126 to 144 beats per minute. Using the old 220 minus Age formula, she would have tried to maintain a target heart rate range of 133 to 152 beats per minute.

The most accurate way to determine your maximum heart rate is with a stress test, administered by a health professional taking into account your gender, weight, age, resting heart rate and other personal factors.

For most people, you can estimate your target heart rate for exercise as follows:

Beginner/Fat-burning – Similar to a heart rate attained during a brisk walk. You should be breathing harder, but not sweating profusely.

Intermediate/Aerobic – Similar to jogging. You should be breathing hard and sweating, but able to talk. You should be able to continue for 15 to 60 minutes at this pace.

Advanced/Anaerobic – Similar to fast running, but not flat-out sprinting. You will tired after 60 to 120 seconds and need to stop.

Heart Rate Monitors/Fitness Wearables

A heart rate monitor is a helpful tool you can use while you work, as well as when you exercise. At least twice a month at work, wear your heart rate monitor during quiet, morning hours and note your resting heart rate. Check your heart rate after you have been sitting calmly for 15 minutes or more. Check it again a while later. Write down your heart rate each time to track your resting heart rate. You should not have any caffeine or sugar, be under deadline stress, have just walked up stairs or performed other physical activity.

After you know your resting heart rate, check it again after you take a two- or three-minute exercise break, such as desk exercises or walking stairs. Use your heart rate to alert you to a very low physical state or agitated one. If you need to make a tough phone call or difficult presentation, check your heart rate. If it's too rapid, try to lower it with deep breathing.

A healthy resting heart rate for most people is anywhere from 60 to 100 beats per minute, depending on how well conditioned you are. The lower your resting heart rate, the better cardiovascular shape you're in. As you exercise, you resting heart rate might decrease. Make sure to adjust your exercising target heart rate range as you improve.

Take a Treadmill/Stress Test

To get an accurate assessment of your heart health, treat yourself to a professionally administered stress test, often performed on a treadmill. Qualified professionals will assess your cardiopulmonary capacity and stamina and let you know your resting and maximum heart rate, giving you target heart rate ranges for beginner, intermediate and advanced workouts. In addition to evaluating you for exercise, your health professional can determine whether you have an abnormal heart rhythm or have other warning signs of poor heart health.

Physical Activity While Traveling

- Choose hotels with gyms

- Ask if your employer purchases/subsidizes exercise equipment

- Get a physical and a treadmill/stress test.

- Take a paper exercise guide on trips for hotel room workouts.

- Bookmark links to videos of hotel room exercises.

About Exercise Equipment

Wondering what exercise equipment you should use at the gym or buy for your home? Here are some quick details on your different options.

Dumbbells
If you want to build some muscle to help improve your ability to burn more calories throughout the day and perform better physically, consider dumbbells. You can buy dumbbells cheaply at most local sporting goods stores. You do not need a dumbbell set, and may be able to get away with only one. Dumbbells are an excellent choice for circuit-training workouts.

Women should choose a weight of 2.5 pounds to 10 pounds, depending on whether you will be using them during aerobic workouts or using them during a portion of some workouts. Men should start with 10-pound dumbbells or higher for cardio workouts, and heavier weights for bodybuilding. The key is to choose a weight you can continue to use without having to stop your workout after only a few minutes. As you build your strength, you can buy heavier dumbbells.

Kettlebells

A kettlebell looks like a bowling ball with a handle. You can use a kettlebell in much the same way you use dumbbells. The handle makes the kettlebell unstable, since the weight does not have a uniform shape. This requires you to recruit your core muscles during exercises to keep yourself balanced, adding another benefit to your exercises. To choose the right weight kettlebell, determine if you can use the weight for 15 minutes or more without having to stop your workout due to sore muscles.

An excellent way to build muscle, burn calories and improve your core all at once is with kettlebell swinging. Start with the kettlebell on the floor in front of you, between your legs, which should be about shoulder width apart. Squat down, sticking your buttocks backward, lowering yourself while you keep your torso straight and your eyes straight ahead.

Grasp the kettlebell with one or two hands, depending on the weight you are using. Swing the kettlebell straight up to shoulder or head height, using a simultaneous upward leg drive and forward hip thrust. Let the ball fall back down between your legs, keeping it off the floor as you swing it up and down over and over again.

Make sure you keep a straight torso and use your legs, hips and arms — not your back — do swing the kettlebell. You can take frequent breaks during kettlebell swinging as long as you keep them short and keep your heart rate elevated throughout the workout.

Home Gyms and Weight Machines

You can use home gyms and weight machines with low resistance settings to create cardio and weight-loss workouts. While you may think of these machines as bodybuilding tools, if you use very little weight while performing the exercises, you can raise your heart rate for longer periods while you work your muscles. The key is to find a weight or resistance setting for each exercise that doesn't fatigue you to failure. Use this type of gym equipment to create cardio and circuit-training workouts.

Cardio Machines

Cardio machines include such equipment as treadmills, ellipticals, rowers, Gazelles, exercise bikes and other machines that let you exercise at your aerobic heart rate for many minutes. They can be extremely beneficial for beginners, intermediates or advanced exercisers. They can also be expensive, boring, limiting and cause repetitive stress injuries.

Even if you find an exercise machine you like using and will continue to use, you'll limit the benefit of exercise you get over time as your body adapts to the limited muscles you use on one machine. You can also cause bodily stress by working the same muscles, tendons and ligaments the same way over and over.

It's best to use a variety of cardio machines, switching which machine you use each workout, or moving from machine to machine every 10 minutes during a workout. If you want to buy a cardio machine for your home or office, use it in conjunction with other workout methods, such as calisthenics or circuit training with dumbbells or resistance bands.

Chapter Summary

- Boosting your metabolism several times each day helps your brain function better.

- You don't need to do vigorous exercise in the office to benefit from physical activity.

- Get up from your desk for a few minutes each 60-90 minutes.

- Walk stairs each day.

- Learn two or three easy desk exercise to do every hour or so.

- For outside-of-work exercise, work out at any pace you can sustain for 30 minutes or more without pain.

- Choose exercise you enjoy doing, rather than "the best" workout.

- Add HIIT (vs. cardio) to your workouts.

- Add some resistance to workouts.

- Buy and use a heart rate monitor.

- Take a treadmill stress test.

- Create a simple workout area in your home.

Chapter 4:
Managing (not Eliminating) Workplace and Home Stress

Stress is not an emotion.

Stress is the physical reactions to your thoughts.

Think about pulling on a piece of plastic until it breaks. Do you notice how the plastic turns white at the point where it's just about to break?

So what is the stress, pulling on the plastic, or the gradual degradation of the plastic that causes it to turn white and break?

If your client threatens to fire you and you begin to get nervous, you might think the client's threat is the stress. What if you tell your client, "I don't care, you're a lousy customer anyway." Then the threat really wasn't stress.

In the first scenario (the one in which you got nervous), the stress was your reaction to the threat and inability to deal with it.

This isn't semantics.

You need to get away from thinking of stress as primarily an emotion or you won't understand and be able to deal with the physical reactions caused by stress that break down your body and reduce your brain functions.

Stress is a specific physical response to our thoughts that puts us into a "fight or flight" state. Stressful situations trigger the release of multiple hormones that affect your central nervous system, muscles, glands and organs and produce specific physiological changes.

Have you ever been driving in your car and then suddenly, a police car turned on its lights behind you? Your first reaction may have been a sudden and slight case of panic. "What did I do?," "What's happening?," "Am I going to get a ticket?"

Your heart rate probably went up. Your hands may have started to shake a bit. Your mouth might have gone dry. You might have started to sweat.

Why did you suddenly have these physical reactions to your thoughts? No one had touched you. Your car hadn't crashed into anything. You were not in any immediate danger . . . yet your body produced physical reactions in response to the thought of being pulled over.

If the police officer ended up not pulling you over and sped around you to go on another call, your heart rate went down, your muscles relaxed and you started breathing deeper.

Do you know why these physical responses happened?

Based on what you are thinking, your brain releases hormones that can make you feel relaxed, tense, excited, nervous, motivated or scared.

When you are stressing, your brain will release adrenaline and/or noradrenaline (also known as epinephrine and norepinephrine), which affect your nervous system. Depending on how long you stress, it will start to produce more cortisol, which has more serious affects.

Stress hormones start out as good guys, giving you the tools you need to cope, such as more blood, oxygen and sugar, to manage the stress.

However, the sustained presence of these hormones in your brain and blood has very serious physical and mental health issues.

Negative short-term physical reactions to stress include:

- Racing heart
- Dry mouth
- Shaking muscles
- Paralysis
- Sweating
- Elevated blood pressure
- Increased alertness
- Digestion problems
- Poor sleep
- Headaches
- Decreased libido
- Increased acne
- Weight gain

A friend of mine who was a nationally recognized, high-powered corporate consultant would start losing her voice once or twice each year. She worked at least six days per week, and 16 hours Monday through Friday.

She thought her voice problem was layringitis caused by talking too much during certain engagements, but it got bad enough that she had to go to a doctor.

The doctor told her that her stressed-out state was causing her stomach to release acids that were literally burning her vocal chords, and if she didn't figure out a way to stop the stress, she'd lose her voice completely.

How are these physical reactions possible? They are primarily due to the release of three primary stress hormones: adrenaline, norepinephrine, and cortisol.

Adrenaline and Norepinephrine
These are the first stress hormones released, raising your metabolism, giving you energy to deal with stress and creating a sense of arousal to get you into the "fight or flight" state.

Cortisol
Cortisol is the main stress hormone. It kicks in within minutes. It helps your body replenish energy stores that are depleted during the stress response. The longer you have elevated cortisol levels, the more physiological and mental problems you'll suffer.

Elevated cortisol levels:
- Interfere with learning and memory (mental "cloudiness" or "brain fog")
- Reduce blood flow to the brain, hurting concentration and memory.
- Lower immune function (more prone to infections)
- Reduce bone density
- Increase weight gain
- Increase blood pressure
- Increase blood cholesterol
- Increase your risk for heart disease
- Increase risk for depression, mental illness
- Lower life expectancy
- Increase appetite and storage of unused nutrients as fat
- Hamper the immune system, making you more prone to infections

Alzheimer's patients with the highest levels of cortisol also had the fastest rates of decline. The Franklin Institute, a center for science education and development, suggests that chronic stress and depletion of dopamine in exchange for hormone flooding creates the internal body environment perfect for Alzheimer's disease, Parkinson's disease, heart disease and cancer in addition to numerous autoimmune disorders that can be disabling.

Negative short-term psychological reactions to stress include:

- Fight or flight
- Depression
- Anxiety
- Irritability
- Anger
- Helplessness

Depending on what is occurring during your workday, your brain will increase the production of specific hormones based on what it thinks you need to cope with the situation. This can have positive or negative affects.

When researchers studied mice—specifically the bullies and those with social aversion in the group—they found that these mice had higher cortisol levels. When the researchers blocked cortisol receptors in these mice, they joined the group again.

If you have to give a speech in front of a roomful of people, you can start to perspire, shake, get dry mouth, stammer or feel dizzy. If you love making sales presentations, your heart rate will rise, you'll feel positive and you'll have extra energy.

If you have high cortisol levels, you might be more likely to be critical of co-workers, be less forgiving of their mistakes and more likely to snap at them. You might stop going to lunch with your co-workers or after-hours social activities. You'll soon develop a reputation for being aloof, a grouch and a jerk.

Many common situations can cause your brain to release stress hormones, including:

- Having to confront, discipline or terminate an employee
- Making a sales call (in person or on the phone)
- Dealing with an irate client or customer
- Public speaking
- Being interviewed by the media
- Facing a deadline
- Dealing with a financial crisis
- Asking for a raise
- Being called into your superior's office for a reprimand

Stressful situations cause short-term physical reactions, while prolonged stress and the release of stress hormones and neurotransmitters over and over again can suppress your immune system, making you more susceptible to colds, flus and other ailments.

One example of stress causing illness is the story of a teenage tennis player who was under loads of stress from her parents wanting her to win. She had to withdraw from multiple competitions because her immune system became suppressed from hormone releases and she frequently became ill with a cold or flu and had to stay home in bed. Another example is the woman previously mentioned executive her lost her voice from stress.

Reducing stress is critical to achieving not only situational peak performance, but also long-term health and productivity.

Identify Stressful Situations

How can you deal with stressful situations that affect you physically?

Don't wait until you face stressful situations to try and respond to them. Write a list of situations you feel cause you to stress. These could include regular occurrences, such as sales calls, employee reviews, deadlines or public speaking.

If you can identify stressful situations you experience, you can create ways to minimize, avoid or deal with them. Dealing with stress successfully requires a proactive, not reactive approach.

Stress me once, shame on you. Stress me over and over again, shame on me. Don't accept the fact that certain situations stress you out and that they are just part of doing business. Even if you can't eliminate them, you can minimize their impact on your performance, productivity and long-term health.

If you're a Millennial, you might be more comfortable communicating with co-workers, clients, vendors and other via text or email. If you can't be enthusiastic and look people in the eye during face-to-face, one-on-one meetings, or during staff meetings or client presentations, you might have a fear of intimacy. This often results with people who grew up communicating digitally using social media, gaming, texting and email.

Practice speaking with people face to face. Start by having more lunches and dinners with friends. Have friends over for a dinner party you host, rather than just to watch a movie or game. Go to a concert or ball game.

If interacting with people professionally stresses you out, start easing into this process by interacting with people socially, then making an effort to do so more at work.

Prepare/Rehearse

Decide if you can identify when stressful situations you have pinpointed will occur before they occur. This will help you learn to identify stressful situations as soon as they begin to happen.

Being able to identify and recognize stressful situations will help you prepare for them in advance. When stress starts to occur, you can then have a plan in place to immediately and successfully cope with it.

Once you have identified stressful situations, develop ways to deal with them and practice these techniques in advance. These techniques can be as simple as controlling your breathing.

Controlling your breathing can help lower your heart rate. Take a deep breath and hold it for two or three seconds. Slowly let it out. You should feel a release of the physical tension in your shoulders and a decreased heart rate. Try this now.

Breathe through your nose to pull deeper breaths into your lungs.

Try this now.

Another technique you can use to combat stress caused by another person is to pause before you verbally respond. Count to two before you answer a question, accusation or other stressful verbal communication. This will help you become proactive as you answer, rather than reactive.

Practice receiving a question or comment, and then mentally counting to two before you answer, even if you know the answer you want to give. You might tap your finger against your thigh twice, lick your lips or just mentally count, "One thousand, two thousand," before you answer.

Another technique to help reduce the effects of stress is to avoid sugar and caffeine if you are going into a stressful situation. Eat more complex carbohydrates, which helps with serotonin production, which can help relax you.

If you can visit a humorous website, watch a comedy clip. Laughter requires more oxygen, which has a therapeutic effect on your body, and deep laughter can stimulate serotonin production in your muscles. It also releases norepinephrine, the "feel good" hormone.

When you're nervous, you may avoid eye contact. Your employee, client or prospective customer may notice your eyes darting up and down and around the room. If you can't look someone in the eye when you are under stress, focus on their nose or lips to keep your eyes centered. If you can make eye contact, be aware of your nerves and make sure you maintain your eye contact.

Practice the following techniques to respond to stressful, person-to-person situations:

- Place your hands on your hips as a positive show of confidence.
- Look into the other person's eyes.
- Uncross your arms and legs if you have crossed them.
- Sit or stand up straight.
- Pause for two seconds before responding verbally—don't talk over someone. You will seem in better control.

Recognize and React

Are you a pushover? Can employees come in late without penalty? Do you agree to deadline extension requests, or allow missed deadlines without consequences?

When you cave in because you are too afraid to hurt someone's feelings or can't deal with conflict or confrontation, you can carry your embarrassment, frustration or other negative feelings with you. You can lose self-confidence or self-esteem, which will continue to nag at you. You can carry anger toward a particular co-worker, supplier, vendor, client or your employer.

Learn to deal with conflict, which can be as easy as saying, "No" or giving a subordinate or co-worker an option that contains a carrot and stick to change behavior. For example, you can extend a deadline, but the employee will need to stay late to finish the job. If you give a deadline, assume it won't be met and be prepared with a response.

You can also try to avoid stress. Don't wait for bad news. If you have assigned deadlines, check in with your client, vendor or employee shortly before the deadline to get a report on their status. Ask if they will make their deadline, if they are facing any problems and if they need any help from you.

Quite often, someone who misses a deadline knows in advance they won't make the deadline. Instead of alerting the proper people, they wait until deadline to inform you of the situation. Let people you give deadlines to know they need to let you know as soon as possible if they might miss the deadline. Set a date to check in with them or assign status reports.

Read your list of potentially stressful situations and learn to recognize when they might occur. Learn to implement the stress-reducing techniques you've practiced as soon as you recognize stressful situations.

Many responses to stress can make you look weak or guilty, even if you are not. Simple body language habits you may not notice can include things such as crossing your arms and legs, slouching, avoiding eye contact, putting your hands in your pockets or tugging on a piece of clothing or jewelry. More obvious responses include stammering, mumbling and sweating.

To deal with bullies, the best defense (when they are wrong) is a strong offense. Learn to recognize when you are on the defensive and use body language and other techniques to get into a controlled state; now, you can become offensive.

For example, your first reaction to a confrontation might be to take a deep breath, let it out, then pause before you answer. Once you have controlled yourself, uncross your legs, place both feet on the floor and sit up straight if you are sitting. If you're standing, uncross your arms and place your hands on your hips. Look the other person in the eyes.

Be careful that you don't present a combative body language, such as leaning into someone, moving into their personal space or pointing your finger at them. Find the right balance of confidence and control to let the other person know you are not afraid of them, and that they are not "winning."

There are times you want to project a neutral stance, especially with a client or superior. You don't want to be defensive, but you don't want to be antagonistic. You want to project an image that there is no stress in the room and that there's no problem. You are oblivious to any negativity. If someone sees you are relaxed, this can let the other person relax. They might rethink their perception of the situation if you are not negative about it.

Sitting slouched with your arms crossed sends a negative, defensive message. Sitting up straight, making eye contact, speaking in a loud voice and leaning forward can send an offensive message. Leaning back in your chair with your hands on your thighs can send a relaxed, neutral message.

Remember, no one can cause you stress—but you can let them cause you stress. If you think a situation is stressful, then it is. If you decide that you are not defensive, you will be offensive.

Dealing with Ongoing Stress

If you have a stressful job, the long-term physical effects can become serious. You can develop an ulcer, high blood pressure, sleep and digestive problems and a suppressed immune system. These can lead to depression, anxiety, anger, lack of focus and eventually increase your risk of heart attack and stroke.

Some self-help gurus suggest you learn techniques to avoid or minimize stress. Other experts suggest you subject yourself to controlled stress, such as competitive sports or rigorous exercise, to learn to handle more stress.

If you are under stress for long periods of time, you'll need more than just on-the-job techniques to deal with them.

Adequate sleep and exercise are two key factors in addressing stress. As the sleep chapter of this book revealed, sleep helps reduce cortisol levels, repairs cell damage and provides other physical and mental benefits that can help you reduce the effects of stress.

Sports = Controlled Stress

Your thoughts affect not only your physiology, but also your actions. You often make bad decisions under stress.

Consider the tennis player who is facing set point and misses her first serve. What is her response to this pressure? In many cases, she will double fault, and if so, she will probably hit her second serve into the net, rather than long or wide. Why?

Because tennis players toss their balls lower when they are trailing Love-40 or 15-40 than when they are leading 40-love or 40-15.

Why do tennis players this? Because a high toss requires you to reach higher and get on your toes or off your feet to go after the ball. When tennis players are nervous, they keep the ball close to their bodies and stay on their heels so they can control the ball better. They don't go for it . . . because they are under stress.

So, the thought of being down set point and having a second serve creates mental stress. This mental stress results in physiological reactions, such as a higher heart rate and weak muscles. This physical reaction to stress causes you to make bad decisions (a low toss), and leads to failure (double fault).

Sports repeatedly puts you under <u>controlled</u> stress (e.g., double faulting or missing a putt won't cost your company thousands or millions of dollars). It teaches you to recognize stress. It shows you what your reactions to stress are. And it repeatedly gives you the opportunity to practice addressing your stress and using techniques to minimize it.

Well-coached tennis players recognize a high-pressure serving situation. They take something off the serve and get a first serve in, rather than taking a chance on facing the stress of a second serve.

They toss their balls higher and decide that if they are going to miss, they are going to miss with confidence, not out of fear. They learn to take a deep breath, hold it, and release it slowly to lower their heart rate.

Many nervous golfers miss their putts by hitting short, yelling, "Hit it Alice!" after they miss. They miss short out of fear, not wanting to hit the ball too hard and miss long, which can result in a longer, more difficult second putt.

Playing sports helps you learn to experience, recognize, control and overcome stress. Playing competitive sports triggers the release of cortisol and can help you learn to control your anger and fear during games and matches.

If you can learn to count to 10 or bite your tongue when a teammate or opponent is getting on your nerves, you'll be able to transfer that skill when co-workers or clients irritate you.

In addition to reducing or avoiding stress in your life, you should learn how to handle stress, and more of it. Sports allows you to voluntary experience stress in a controlled environment without the pressure of the many negatives associated with business stress.

For example, the score in a sports game or match puts stress on you. Targets, such as goals, boundaries, receivers and holes put stress on you. Outcomes, such winning or breaking 100 during a golf game put <u>controlled</u> pressure on you.

These are examples of stresses that challenge your mind and body in positive ways. The most mentally tough competitors in sports or business love challenges and pressure. Participating in sports helps you expose yourself to pressure, learn to deal with it, learn not to fear it and learn techniques for overcoming it.

What is "first hole jitters" in golf? It's the nervousness many golfers feel when they hit their first shot of the day. Why would your first drive cause you to be more nervous than any other shot during your round? Because you want to start well and not make a fool of yourself in front of your associates or friends.

Your fellow players are watching you to see how their afternoon with you is going to go. If you top the first ball or slice it way into the woods, you know they will be thinking, "Oh great! I'm stuck with this hack all afternoon."

Even though you use the same swing to hit your first tee shot that you'll be using over and over the next 17 holes, you are still nervous. But it's only because you put this pressure on yourself. This is an excellent example of facing stress in a controlled situation and learning how to overcome it.

Participating in sports, as simple as playing golf, racquetball, tennis or three-on-three basketball, provides you the important benefit of being able to repeatedly expose yourself to stress in controlled situations so you can learn to overcome it.

Traffic and Stress

Traffic can cause you significant stress each day, making you arrive at the office in a tense, bad mood. It can also maintain or raise your stress levels after work, making you nervous and irritable when you get home.

Think about why you get upset in traffic.

In the morning, does traffic make you late for work? At night, does someone cutting you off or driving slowly make you lean on the horn? Are you listening to talk radio?

Traffic and bad drivers can't stress you out. You can let them stress you out, but if you learn to accept the inevitable situations that arise in traffic over and over again, realize that bad traffic won't kill you, and refuse to let other drivers or slow traffic drive you crazy, you can eliminate significant stress in your life each day.

If you are in management, consider de-stressing your employees by offering parking options that let them park close to your building in a safe, easy-access environment. Offer to buy rail or bus passes, set up a carpool van or give employees who carpool free and covered parking.

Don't listen to talk radio that upsets you during a commute, even if you agree with the host's political views.

Exercise

Exercise helps you deal with stress differently than playing sports does. Exercise burns energy, raises your heart rate and releases brain hormones that can elevate your mood. Unlike sports, exercise has none of the scoring, target or other performance pressure that can negatively affect your mood.

This is why, unlike athletes during games and matches, joggers and weightlifters rarely throw their equipment around and smash things while working out.

Exercise also helps you sleep better, a key tool in the fight against stress.

If you are in a position to add a wellness program to your workplace, help your workers reduce stress by offering free or reduced-priced gym memberships, personal trainer consultations or lectures, weight-loss contests, rebates on exercise equipment or an on-site fitness room.

Meditation and Mindfulness

The term meditation has been around for centuries and became more well-known to consumers via the Beatles in the late 1960s and early 1970s. Mindfulness is a newer concept being promoted for corporate wellness.

These practices help you relax, reduce mental stress and lower your metabolism. They try to help you put your life in perspective and understand what's really important.

Both can be very helpful for reducing stress.

However, re-thinking your priorities can lead to decreased workplace motivation, according to researchers who published, "Mindfulness Meditation Impairs Task Motivation but Not Performance." The researchers found that meditation does not decrease performance (and actually increased task focus by eliminating stressors), but can reduce drive.

If you practice meditation, be aware of its effect on your view of your work. It's a good thing to develop a healthy set of priorities that allow you to place less importance on menial task and give you the confidence to delegate. Just make sure you don't begin "blowing off" projects because you think they're not important in the grand scheme of life.

Get Personal Support

Don't try to deal with a high-pressure job or long-term negative situation by yourself. Even if you simply talk about your problems and vent to a family member or friend, you can release some of your tension.

If you don't have a specific, negative situation with which you're dealing, but your job is generally stressful, spend time with other people outside of work.

Instead of exercising by yourself or watching TV at home, set up a tennis or racquetball match. Work out at a gym with a partner, hire a personal trainer for 30 minutes or drop in on an exercise class. Go out for dinner and drinks with a group of friends. Offer to babysit for friends. Pets can provide positive energy; consider pet sitting for a friend or walking an elderly neighbor's dog.

In some instances, you'll want to talk about work, such as with a partner, sibling or parent. In other situations, you'll want to simply spend time with others to take your mind off work.

Alcohol, Tobacco and Drugs

Alcohol, tobacco and drugs aren't the main culprits in substance abuse. It's the reasons people use them that are the real problem.

You probably never hear people say, "My job is going great. I have plenty of money. My kids are wonderful. I have lots of friends. I need to get wasted!"

People lean on substances to help them deal with stress caused by work, relationships, money problems and other issues. If you have more than a social drink or two at a party, a glass of wine with dinner or are still smoking pot or using cocaine into adulthood, you may want to ask yourself why.

Even if you are not addicted to any substance, it might be a good idea to catalogue any you use and ponder scenarios in which you might turn to them for more than recreation.

If your work scenario suddenly becomes desperate, or if your marriage goes south, do you know which substance you might most likely reach for to help relax you? If so, it's a good idea to identify some red flags that will tell you that you may be headed toward substance abuse.

Do you begin drinking in the morning or alone? Do you spend more money on drugs than normal? Do you smoke only at work? These are signs you may be using substances to deal with stress, rather than trying to eliminate the stress.

Some studies have suggested (not shown) that alcohol consumption can reduce stress. The thinking is that alcohol is a depressant and can relax you. Is this just a temporary treatment for stress without eliminating the cause?

A famous study on red wine "found" that the ingredient resveratrol helped reduce heart disease. That study was later found to have included falsified data, but that "finding" is still being spread among consumers today.

Red wine and resveratrol might have some legitimate benefits, but do you really want to rely on alcohol to keep you healthy, rather than eliminating the causes of your stress?

To-Do Lists

Do you ever feel out of control at work? Lack of organization, planning and tracking deprives you of a clear picture of where you need to go and how you are doing.

To-do lists are an excellent way to add control to your life. They tell you exactly what you need to get done and let you know how you are doing with a quick glance. They can alleviate stress by showing you that you are, in fact, getting things done.

To-do lists can also motivate you to stay on track by reminding you that you have unfinished work. This can help prevent you from starting new projects that can wait until later, fooling around on the computer or working too slowly.

To-do lists can also add stress to your life if you create unrealistic lists or set unrealistic deadlines for completing them.

Tips for Reducing and Managing (not Eliminating) Stress

- Get sufficient sleep and take naps
- Exercise three or more times per week
- Keep a daily journal
- Talk with people about everyday stresses
- Listen to relaxing music to reduce cortisol levels
- Avoid work and stressful TV shows at least one hour before bed
- Organize your day and week with a to-do list
- Reduce your intake of coffee, cigarettes, tea, beer, wine and soda.
- Increase real (not digital) interpersonal connectivity
- Reduce your media time
- Turn off talk radio
- Add humor (comedy clubs, TV shows, videos)
- Have the confidence to delegate work

Stress Questions

The more of these questions you answer, "Yes," the more likely you are creating stress in your life.

Do you feel you are always late or behind schedule?

Do you feel disorganized?

Are you still angry about things that have happened in the past?

Are you upset with friends, family members or business associates who do not know you are upset with them?

Do you feel you do any emotional eating?

Do you dislike delegating, preferring to handle tasks yourself?

Do you get irritated or angry easily or frequently?

Do you share your feelings with someone, or keep to yourself?

Do you exercise regularly?

Do you regularly get enough sleep?

Are you impatient with vendors, clients, or co-workers?

Do you wait until deadline to finish projects?

Do you feel your job is in jeopardy?

Do you have financial problems?

Do you have relationship problems?

Do you use alcohol or cigarettes to relieve stress?

Chapter Summary

- Don't think of stress as an emotion—think of it as the damaging results of negative emotions.

- Your thoughts stimulate the production of various chemicals that affect your body.

- Write a list of situations you know cause you stress.

- Identify signs that tell you a stressful situation is coming.

- Prepare responses to stressful situations.

- Rehearse your reaction to stressful situations.

- Use sports to expose yourself to control stressed and to practice stress-reducing techniques.

- Take a deep breath, hold it, and let it go slowly. Take a deep breath through your nose.

- Exercise at the end of a stressful day.

- Learn to mentally deal with traffic.

- Use family, friends and pets as stress-release valves.

- Analyze your use of alcohol, tobacco and drugs to determine when and why you use them.

- Use to-do lists to organize your day.

Chapter 5: Why Routines Help

Have you ever noticed that the top professional athletes bounce a tennis ball the same number of times before each serve, or waggle the golf club the same way before each tee shot or spin the basketball the same way before bouncing it the same number of times before each free throw?

Athletes know that if you perform the same routine or ritual before each shot, it sends a message to your brain to move your muscles in a way that creates the optimal shot.

Top athletes even perform the same game-day routines before they even get to the stadium, down to the order in which they shave, shower, have breakfast and get dressed.

One of the practices high-performing workers can adopt to reduce stress and increase peak performance is to add rituals, routines or habits to their daily routines.

This starts with how you get up in the morning and the order in which you perform tasks to get ready to leave the house.

It can include how you commute to work.

It should include how you order, organize and manage your day in the workplace.

It should include how you commute back home and how you order their regular evening activities.

Become Proactive, Not Reactive

Routines are not OCD practices. They help get you on autopilot so you can perform tasks quicker and more efficiently.

With athletes, rituals trigger the brain to send specific messages via the central nervous system to your muscles for the best physical performance.

They can also stimulate information stored in the brain so that you can repeat previous successes.

For example, champion athletes often have a game-day ritual that they use every competition day. Some eat, then shower and dress. Others shower, then dress and eat.

This type of routine creates patterns than can you help manage a lack of time in the morning and reduce stress.

What do you listen to in the car on the way to and from work? Is it talk radio? Don't listen to it.

How do you start each day? Do you eat breakfast at your desk? Check emails first? Surf the net for the morning news and sports scores?

Decide what is the least-stressful, most productive routine for starting your day (e.g., checking emails) and then start your day that way each day.

Add an Extra Ritual for Important Workdays

Are there certain days that are more important to you than others?

- Surgery

- Sales presentations to clients

- Closing argument or witness cross examination

- Staff meetings

- Employee reviews

If so, think about adding one or two extra routines to those days to send a message to your brain, "This is a day I need to perform at my peak. It's different than any other day. I need to be more alert and focused today than on most other days."

You might simply have a specific breakfast or lunch, wear a certain outfit or just change the order of a few of your normal daily routines. However you do it, send yourself a signal that today is a special day and you want to perform at your absolute best.

If this works, why not do this every day? Because it's virtually impossible to be at your absolute peak 24/7. It would also be exhausting to be in a fight-or-flight state all day, every day.

It's important to create habits and routines that you use on a daily basis to perform at or near your best, but it's OK to create a special habit or routine to make sure that certain days even more hyper-focused.

Create Post-Work Routines

What do you do after you get home in the evening? Think about creating a home routine that helps you decompress, relax and reduce stress. Non-work related chores such as taking the dog out, making dinner, playing with the kids, doing dishes, cleaning around the house and getting ready for the next day can be stressful if they bombard you with no apparent rhyme or reason.

List the activities you regularly have after you get home from work and think about putting at least some of them into a routine that helps you take control of your evenings, rather than being reactive. Activities to include in a home routine might include:

- Opening snail mail
- Changing clothes
- Exercising
- Eating
- Watching TV
- Waking a pet
- Cooking dinner
- Cleaning the kitchen
- House chores

You don't need to ruthlessly regulate your evening activities, but when it comes to eating, exercising and getting read for bed, try adding some rituals.

Chapter 6: What's Your Work/Home Air Quality Like?

Sick home/sick building syndrome is on the rise.

Energy Star home products like energy efficient windows and doors, and tightly sealed hi-tech buildings contribute to fewer hours spent in fresh air.

If you work in an office and have a modern home, for most of the day, you might be:

- Sealed in your home while you sleep and while you get ready for work in the morning
- Sealed in your car on the way to work
- Sealed in your work building
- Sealed in your car on the way home from work
- Sealed in your homes again in the evening

More chemicals and toxins are found in:

- Furniture
- Flooring
- Drywall
- Wall coverings and coatings
- Electronics
- Clothing
- Vehicles
- HVAC systems

Thanks to advances in technology, our homes and buildings are more energy efficient. They keep hot air from leaking into our homes and offices during the warm months as we're spending money to cool them. They keep cold air out and prevent the air we've just paid to warm from escaping.

What else happens?

We trap all of the coughs, sneezes, dust, toxins, gases and other harmful air contaminants in the house, vehicle or workplace with us.

Think about sleeping all night in a house with energy efficient windows and doors, then getting ready for work the next morning as your spouse, partner, kids or pets are getting ready for their days.

You then get into your car, roll up the windows and turn on the air conditioning or heater.

You park in the workplace garage, get into an elevator, then go to work in an office you share with dozens of other people and inhale not only what they're exhaling, but whatever else is coming out of the air ducts, and electronic devices in the building.

You then get back into your home, drive home with the windows closed, and then finally enter your energy efficient home for the rest of the evening and through the next morning.

Air Duct Cleaning Facts & Fiction

If you haven't had your home or office air ducts inspected and cleaned for a number of years, it's probably a good idea to do so. There might be a buildup of mold, critters' nests or other issues.

According to the National Institutes of Health and U.S. Environmental Protection Agency, there is no proven benefit to having your home or workplace air ducts cleaned every year. In fact, doing so might actually stir up contaminants that would not otherwise harm you and spread them throughout the structure.

Tips for Improving Air Quality

- Replace your home air filters every 90 days.

- Have your home HVAC unit inspected to make sure it's working properly if you haven't done so during the last few years. Consider annual inspections.

- Have your air ducts inspected and cleaned if you haven't done so during the last few years.

- Try a humidifier. Keep the filter and water basin clean.

- Add screens to your front door and one or two windows per floor so you can open your doors and windows to let stale air out and fresh air in.

- Rotate the direction of ceiling fans twice each year.

    - Clockwise in winter to push warm air down.

    - Counterclockwise in summer to create a cooler airflow.

- Clean ceiling fan blades every month or so.

- Don't clean mold stains on walls or tile with bleach. That only cleans the stain. To kill the roots of mold that live under surfaces, look for an EPA-approved mold removal product.

Talk to your employer about how it's managing workplace air quality.

Get Outside More Often

- Ask your employer to set up an outdoor lunch/break area.

- Have dinner on your home deck or patio more often.

- Make phone calls outdoors.

- Bring your laptop outdoors.

- Take a walk after dinner.

- Exercise outdoors.

- Offer to walk a neighbor's dog.

- Do more yard work.

Chapter 7: Managing the Flu (You're Going to Get it)

If you work in an office or fly commercially, you have a good chance of getting the flu each year.

After seniors and children, office workers may be the next most likely group to catch the flu annually, which not only whacks millions of people each year with considerable pain and illness, but kills thousands, as well. As much as 20 percent of the U.S. population gets the flu annually, with an estimated 200,000 Americans requiring hospitalization and thousands dying.

And we're not talking about the type of flu we got as kids that let us stagger into class or the office while fighting off our 24-hour bug. Today's flu strains are much more serious and are likely to badly slam you for a minimum of three days or last as long as a week. And there is more than one strain floating around each year.

You also may not be able to work from home as you suffer from headaches, high fever, sore throat, vomiting, diarrhea, deep coughing, chills and sore joints. If you're an attorney who bills $200 an hour, 10 hours a day, a three-day bout with the flu can cost your firm $6,000. If you make a $100,000 annual salary, you could lose more than $1,400 in paid time off if you're sick three days.

A $20 flu shot is conceivably the biggest no-brainer health investment a working professional can make. Additionally, it's a good idea to spend some money on flu meds and foods before you get sick — once you're very ill, you may not be able to get out of bed and go to the store for what you need, dragging your flu out longer than necessary and being sicker than you need to be.

The Basics

What can you do once you get the flu? First, it's important to differentiate between treating the actual flu and reducing its symptoms.

According to expert sources like the Mayo Clinic and Centers for Disease Control and Prevention, the best way to treat he flu is simply to get plenty of rest and drink lots of fluids. This doesn't mean you can't do a variety of things to help alleviate symptoms and reduce your pain and suffering while you have the flu.

Some natural treatments make common sense, but may backfire, so it's best you consult a physician before trying any that go beyond rest, hydration and over-the-counter meds.

For example, mothers are told not to try and break a child's fever when he as the measles or chicken pox, because a fever is your body's way of trying to naturally kill germs by "burning" or "baking" them. Taking this logic, you might want to raise your thermostat, put on sweats, pile on the covers and try to raise your body temperature to kill your flu. However, this can lead to dehydration or a more severe fever, which can lead to brain damage.

Think of your brain like a raw egg. When you put it into a hot pan, the protein-rich yoke turns from bright yellow to a dull yellow as it heats up. When your protein-rich brain reaches a certain temperature, you can do permanent damage.

On the other hand, you can try to reduce your body temperature to feel better, lowering your home temperature, lying on top of your covers, drinking iced liquids, taking a tepid bath or using cold compresses on your forehead, ankles, knees, wrists and elbows. This may make you feel better, but fights your body's attempts to address your flu cause.

Before you attempt to regulate your body temperature, contact your personal physician, local doc-in-the-box or your pharmacy and ask for advice. Don't trust websites that seem to be authoritative unless they are connected with a hospital, university or government agency. Even then, you might misinterpret the data, so it's best to talk with a professional.

Some believe that light exercise can help you overcome the flu, raising your body temperature and releasing positive hormones. Depending on how severe your symptoms are, this could weaken you, and you might fall or otherwise injure yourself while exercising. While getting out of bed and walking around may help you clear your head and shake off some grogginess, you probably shouldn't get on an exercise machine without talking to a health professional first.

What to Eat?

While you can choose foods that contain specific vitamins and minerals to try and target illnesses, once you have the flu, food and medicines, including much-touted vitamin C, won't cure you. Eating a balance of mild foods that won't upset your stomach and provide you with a good mix of complex carbohydrates, lean protein, vitamins and minerals is a sensible approach to eating when you have the flu, since it will help boost your immune system.

Fruits and fruit juices are a good source of healthy vitamins and minerals and contain significant amounts of water, helping you stay hydrated. They should not be your sole source of nutrition while you're sick, since you'll need your carbs and protein. Avoid fruit juices that are mostly water, sweeteners, additives and preservatives. Fresh or canned fruit are better choices than most commercial fruit juices. Bananas and kiwis are good sources of potassium, an important electrolyte you lose through sweating, vomiting and diarrhea.

Hot soups are another good choice when you have the flu, since they are also water-based and can provide you with carbs, proteins, vitamins and minerals. Soups can help clear congestion because of the steam rising off the dish. Researchers aren't exactly sure why, but chicken soup seems to have an additional benefit beyond other hot liquids in helping reduce mucus production and inflammation.

If you are having a serious problem with congestion, avoid dairy products, which can increase mucus production.

Good carb choices include rice, dry toast, soda crackers, tortillas, mashed potatoes and oatmeal.

If you have vomiting or diarrhea, avoid heavy, spicy foods. Stick with soda crackers, ginger ale, consommé or broth, mashed potatoes and gelatin. Doctors often recommend the BRAT diet when you have the flu – bananas, rice, applesauce and toast. These foods are easily digestible if you're having stomach problems. Fruit and fruit juice may seem mild, but can have citric acid, which can cause stomach problems.

Sports Drinks

When you have the flu, you lose not only water, but also electrolytes, such as salt, potassium and magnesium. Have you ever had very thin saliva with a tinny taste? If so, you're probably lacking in electrolytes. Sports drinks like Gatorade are specifically designed not only to hydrate you, but also to reduce the electrolytes you lose through sweat. When you're sick, you lose more electrolytes through vomiting and diarrhea. Consider drinking a sports drink that provides you with carbohydrates and electrolytes.

Stay away from coffee, tea and caffeinated drinks that can act as diuretics and further dehydrate you.

Other Tips

Medicate
Don't take aspirin. Instead, relieve aches and pain with over-the-counter products that contain ibuprofen and acetaminophen, found in medications like Tylenol, Advil, and Motrin. Try lozenges to help your sore throat and syrups and drinks made to help reduce congestion.

Gargle
Gargle with warm salt water. You can immediately reduce the pain of a sore throat with a salt gargle.

Sit Up
Prop yourself up if you have a headache or congestion. This will help your sinuses drain better than if you lie flat.

Shower
A warm shower will relax your muscles and the steam will help decongest you. Turn your bathroom into a sauna by running the shower with the door closed. If you have a severe fever, be careful of raising your body temperature even further with a hot shower or bath.

Spit
When you cough up liquid, don't swallow it again. Your body is trying to get rid of it. Keep a container near your bed so you can discharge any phlegm or mucus that comes up. Don't keep this near you for days on end — rinse the container out each time you get up.

Blow
Blow your nose gently by doing so slowly, one nostril at a time, rather than by pressing against both nostrils and trying to use lots of pressure.

Plug
Use nose plugs. Constantly sniffling mucus that is running from your nose back into your sinuses can increase the pressure in your head. Take a toilet paper square and rip it in half. Rip the remaining piece in half and roll the two pieces into small balls. Place them in your nose and let them catch any running mucus. These can last for hours or may need to be replaced frequently, depending on how fast your nose is running.

If you put these in when you sleep, they can help you sleep peacefully for many hours; however, you'll be breathing through your mouth the entire time and may experience a sore throat when you awake. A quick salt-water garlic will help alleviate this soreness.

Chapter Summary

- Businesspeople are a high-risk group for the flu. Millions of Americans get the flu each year, with more than 200,000 hospitalized and thousands of death.

- You cannot cure the flu, only treat it and reduce some symptoms.

- Rest and fluids are the best two ways to treat the flu.

- You can reduce many symptoms with nutrition, over-the-counter meds and a few other tips for making yourself more comfortable.

- Have flu meds available in your home before you get sick; once you're very sick, you aren't likely to get out of bed and go to the store.

- Eat mild foods that give you a good mix of complex carbs, lean protein and vitamins and minerals.

- Some sports drinks replace electrolytes you lose sweating, vomiting and going to the bathroom.

- Don't try to raise or lower your body temperature without talking to a doctor first.

- Gargle with warm salt water to relieve a sore throat.

- Don't fly or go into work for at least two days after your fever breaks.

Tips for Dealing with a Hangover

While you can't cure a morning after with a miracle remedy, you can do several things to ease your headache, settle your stomach and decrease your muscle and joint pain.

Re-Hydrate
Alcohol is a diuretic, which means it makes you pee more. When you pee more, you become dehydrated, and this can exacerbate a headache. Rehydrate with water or something more substantive if you've upchucked a time or two. A sports drink with electrolytes can help you replace those you've lost praying to the porcelain god.

Take an Ant-Inflammatory
One of the main causes of a hangover is inflammation, which can lead to the same symptoms as the flu. Taking an anti-inflammatory can help reduce hangover symptoms. Acetaminophen, found in products like Tylenol, can cause liver problems when taken with alcohol. Ibuprofen or aspirin are better anti-inflammatory choices.

Settle Your Stomach
Putting food into your stomach won't "absorb" any alcohol – the booze is already in your bloodstream. However, one of the side effects of a hangover is an upset stomach, so putting some mild food into your gut can settle it a bit. Stick with toast, oatmeal, a banana, yogurt or other simple foods. If you've got leftover pizza sitting on the counter, save it for lunch.

Have a Drink?

Having a drink can temporarily ease the headache that comes with a hangover, but it's not a cure and the headache will probably return.

When you drink alcohol, your brain stops producing glutamate. When you stop drinking and the alcohol starts leaving your body, your brain starts producing glutamate, and the rush of this chemical entering your noggin can cause a headache. Drinking some alcohol will help slow this glutamate production, but only temporarily.

If you just want to delay your headache until later, a little hair of the dog can help. Rather than having a full drink, think about a smaller nip rather than getting a buzz again.

Get Active or Go to Bed

You shouldn't try to perform an intense workout when you're hung over, but getting some low-impact physical activity can help boost your metabolism and reduce the feeling of general grogginess that comes with a hangover. Try a brisk walk outdoors. Pedaling a bike at a moderate speed or doing some light calisthenics are also good choices.

Depending on how much pain you're in, taking the opposite tack (and resting) might be the best idea. After drinking plenty of fluids, get back into bed, get the room as dark as possible, lower the temperature so it's cool in the room and get some Z's.

Putting it All Together

General wellness ≠ performance wellness

There's a difference between general wellness and performance wellness.

General wellness is very important for any businessperson. It helps keep healthy and more productive over the long-term. General wellness, however, doesn't emphasize daily peak performance or create daily routines to specifically improve peak performance each day.

The goal of a performance wellness program plan is to specifically improve efficiency, rather than to avoid decreased productivity. Performance wellness is especially important for high-performing, high-stress employees.

At some point, you need to be scared about what happens long-term if you continue to abuse your body with a lack of sleep, poor diet, lack of physical activity, poor daily air quality and high stress levels.

You're going to age prematurely and struggle during your senior years.

Overworking will permanently damage the quality of your life now because you can't "bank" relationships, love, happiness and peace later in their lives.

At the end of your life, when you're on your deathbed, you don't want to tell the people gathered around your bed, "I don't regret the things I did during my life, I regret the things I didn't do."

Keep this book in the bathroom with a pen or highlighter and make notes in the margins.

After you've read it a few times, take one Sunday evening when things are quiet to write a list of lifestyle and work habit changes you want to make.

After you review your list, you might be surprised at how easy it is to make major improvements to your health, career and happiness with just a little planning.

www.ingramcontent.com/pod-product-compliance
Lightning Source LLC
Chambersburg PA
CBHW071604220526
45469CB00003B/1113